THE NORTH CENTRAL UNITED STATES

WALLACE E. AKIN

Professor of Geography
Drake University

A SEARCHLIGHT ORIGINAL
under the general editorship of

G. EDSEL PEARCY	GEORGE W. HOFFMAN
The Geographer	*Professor of Geography*
U. S. Department of State	**University of Texas**

D. VAN NOSTRAND COMPANY, INC.

PRINCETON, NEW JERSEY

TORONTO   LONDON

MELBOURNE

Van Nostrand Regional Offices:
New York, Chicago, San Francisco

D. Van Nostrand Company, Ltd., *London*

D. Van Nostrand Company (Canada), Ltd., *Toronto*

D. Van Nostrand Australia Pty. Ltd., *Melbourne*

PRINTED IN THE UNITED STATES OF AMERICA

Preface

THIS book is concerned with that part of the continental interior of North America which is bordered by the Appalachians to the east, the Rocky Mountains to the west, the Ohio River and the southern boundary of the states of Missouri, Kansas, and Colorado to the south, and the Canadian boundary to the north. Within this area are the states of Ohio, Indiana, Michigan, Wisconsin, Illinois, Missouri, Iowa, Minnesota, North Dakota, South Dakota, Nebraska, and Kansas, and the eastern parts of Colorado, Wyoming, and Montana.

To the tourist traveling westward across the great expanse of the interior of the United States to reach the scenic attractions of the American West, the area between the Appalachians and the Rockies is often one to pass through as quickly as possible. From the standpoint of productivity this heartland of North America is one of the truly exceptional areas of the earth, an area which contains much of the resource base upon which the United States depends. Here is produced much of the food surplus that has been the concern of agricultural economists and politicians, and the envy of much of the world where agricultural production lags behind population growth.

In a few hours by jet airliner it is possible to observe the visual results of the multiple geographic factors that contribute to the character of the North Central States. As the air traveler crosses the North Central States between the Appalachians and the Rocky Mountains the changes observed on the land below are gradual and subtle. The first impression on leaving the rough, forested hill lands of the Appalachians and entering the broad area of gentle relief which characterizes much of the continental interior, is the rectangular pattern on the land. Field patterns combine with the road system to give the impression of a vast, multicolored chessboard stretching from horizon to horizon, interspersed at intervals with towns and cities.

3

This basic pattern is carried westward to the mountains, but the scale changes. In the east, fields are smaller and towns are more frequent, reflecting the smaller farms and denser population. Westward, as the rainfall decreases and farm operating units increase in size, the density of settlement becomes less and the scale of the chessboard becomes larger.

From a vantage point in the center of the Corn Belt, agriculture may seem to dominate the economy of the North Central States, particularly in the great open spaces west of the Mississippi. However, the great urbanized industrial centers to the east play an equally forceful, although less conspicuous, role in the economy of the area and the nation. Also supplementing the agricultural and industrial productivity are the products of the mines and forests, the vast transportation network, and the numerous other economic activities carried on in the area.

The continental interior of the United States is a remarkable geographic area, in terms both of the resource base inherent in the physical environment and of the utilization of these resources. This book considers the major aspects of the resource base and attempts to show how it has contributed to the development of the North Central States and to the nation as a whole. It not only considers those activities directly related to the exploitation of the physical environment, such as agriculture, forestry, and mining, but it also is concerned with the interaction of all these factors in the total geographic environment.

The author is indebted to his colleagues at Drake University, Dr. Wilfrid G. Richards and Dr. Gerald E. Schultz of the Geography Department, and Dr. Paul Willis of the Political Science Department, for their many helpful suggestions and valuable source materials. To my wife, Peggy, I owe many hours of proofreading and valuable criticism of grammar and style. Special thanks go to Dr. George W. Hoffman for the initial encouragement to write the book, and to Dr. G. Etzel Pearcy for his seemingly unlimited patience in waiting for the manuscript to materialize.

WALLACE E. AKIN

Contents

Tables

5

Maps (following p. 80)

1 *The Nature of the Land*

THE North Central States occupy a major part of the heartland of the North American continent. As treated here, the North Central States are bordered by the eastern boundary of Ohio to the east, the Rocky Mountains to the west, the Canadian border to the north, the Ohio River to the southeast, and the southern boundaries of Missouri, Kansas, and Colorado to the southwest. A large part of the area corresponds to what is generally considered to be the Middle West of the United States, an area not precisely defined in geographic terms. In the east the Appalachian Plateaus of southeastern Ohio have much in common, both physically and culturally, with Appalachia; while along the southern borders of Ohio, Indiana, Illinois, and Missouri, the area is transitional to the South. Along the western margin of the North Central States, the Great Plains environment likewise has much in common with the West.

A combination of favorable topography, climate, and economic function has helped make the North Central States one of the most densely settled and best developed of continental interiors. No comparable area of interior plains can compare with the productivity, both agricultural and industrial, of this part of North America. These advantages include great material resources in the form of soil, climate, and minerals which contribute to a viable economy.

THE PHYSICAL SETTING

The North Central States are a part of the immense area of relatively low relief which extends from the Gulf of Mexico to the Arctic Ocean and from the Rocky Mountains to the Appalachians. Although elevation varies from less than 300 feet at the junction of the Ohio and Mississippi rivers to over 5,000 feet along the western margins of the Great Plains near the Rocky Mountains, only a few areas demonstrate truly rugged topography. Vast areas range in relief from almost flat to gently rolling. As a result, where rainfall permits, a high proportion of the land is under cultivation. Low relief and the absense of major topographic barriers make transportation easy, both on land and on the waterways where long reaches are navigable.

Combined with the favorable topography are other factors of the physical environment, including geology, climate, natural vegetation, and soils, which contribute to the physical basis for the outstanding productivity of this area. These factors occur in a number of combinations that lend uniqueness to the many subdivisions of what, at first glance, might seem to be a homogeneous area.

The Bedrock Geology. The North Central States contain one of the most extensive expanses of sedimentary strata on earth. These rocks consist mainly of limestone, dolomite, sandstone, and shale formed from materials laid down horizontally in ancient seas. The age range of the sedimentary rocks is from Cambrian through Tertiary, with the older formations generally being in the east and the younger in the Great Plains. Subsequent uplifting and gentle warping have produced subdued geological structures, mostly in the form of broad shallow basins and low domes, which cover many thousands of square miles and are hardly perceptible when viewed in a limited area.

In some areas these structures within the sedimentary rocks have formed traps for valuable reservoirs of petroleum and natural gas.

These sedimentary deposits also contain economically important coal beds. In addition to the value of mineral fuels embedded within the sedimentary rocks, the rocks themselves are valuable sources of building materials, agricultural limestone, and ceramic materials. In a few places such as the Superior Uplands, the eastern Ozarks, and the Black Hills, ancient crystalline Precambrian rocks are exposed at the surface. These very old rocks are in some places valuable sources of metallic minerals, one example being that of the Lake Superior iron ore.

Glaciation. One of the most significant geological events that shaped the physical character of the North Central States was continental glaciation. During the last million years a large part of this area has been subjected to at least four major invasions of glacial ice. The earliest glaciation is called the Nebraskan and is almost everywhere covered by younger glacial drifts except where it has been exposed through erosion. Although exact dating is not possible, it is thought that the Nebraskan occurred several hundred thousand years ago. The next glacial advance was the Kansan, which reached to the Missouri River in central Missouri and extended into eastern Kansas south of Topeka. The Kansan glacier is thought to have extended as far south as northern Kentucky east of Louisville. The Kansan advance was followed by the Illinoian, which reached almost to the southern tip of the state of Illinois. The last major glacial advance, the Wisconsin, pushed southward in a series of lobes into eastern Montana, the Dakotas, and the northern parts of Iowa, Illinois, Indiana, and Ohio. This last glacial event came to an end less than 10,000 years ago in the North Central States and was so recent that many of the young glacial features are still clearly visible on the landscape. Because the Wisconsin glacial advance was so recent, several substages are recognized, but they are of interest primarily to the glacial geologist.

Between the major ice advances there were interglacial periods lasting tens of thousands of years during which the climate was undoubtedly as warm as or even warmer than it is today. Evidence of these interglacials can be seen in the deeply weathered soil zones separating superimposed glacial deposits.

The role of glaciation in the formation of the resource base of the North Central States has long been recognized. Where the bedrock consisted of soft limestones and shales, the glaciers ground up much of it, producing the parent material of some of the most productive soils in the world. Where the bedrock was hard crystalline rocks, such as those found in the northern Great Lakes area, the glacial drift is thinner and has given rise to soil materials that are not so good. Also, there is a contrast between the topography of the older drifts, the Kansan and Illinoian, and the Wisconsin glacial drift plains. The old glaciated areas have been dissected in many places into steeply rolling topography, and even where dissection by streams is not complete, a well-integrated drainage pattern is found. In contrast, the Wisconsin glacial areas are generally poorly drained with many peat bogs and lakes, necessitating great expenditures for artificial drainage by tile and ditch before cultivation can succeed. The extra cost of the drainage notwithstanding, these younger drifts south of the crystalline rocks of the Canadian Shield are the basis for some of the best agricultural soils of the United States.

South of the Wisconsin glacial boundary the old glacial drifts are mantled throughout much of their area by deep accumulations of wind-deposited silt called *loess*. The younger silt is believed to have been deposited during the Wisconsin glaciation and is commonly called Wisconsin loess. This loess forms the parent material for some of the best soils of the old drift plains, although in some areas where the clay content is high these soils are not so productive. Some loess deposits are found outside the area of glaciation, particularly in the Great Plains and along the Mississippi River south of the glacial boundary.

The Rivers. By far the major portion of the North Central States is drained by the Mississippi-Ohio-Missouri system. To the east the

Ohio River forms the southern boundary of the area, and its northern tributaries drain southeastern Illinois and all but the northern margins of Ohio and Indiana. The upper Mississippi River and its lesser tributaries drain most of Illinois, Wisconsin, and Minnesota, the northeastern two-thirds of Iowa, and the northeastern portion of Missouri. The Missouri River drains almost all of the northern and part of the central Great Plains to the upper Mississippi River, with the exception of southeastern Colorado and southern Kansas, which are drained through the Arkansas River to the lower Mississippi.

The relatively small part of the North Central States outside the Mississippi drainage system falls into two areas, both of which drain northward rather than south to the Gulf of Mexico. In the east, in areas bordering the Great Lakes, drainage is into the lakes and thence to the North Atlantic by way of the St. Lawrence River. To the west of the Great Lakes, in northern Minnesota and northern North Dakota, the drainage is northward to Hudson Bay through the Red River and Lake Winnipeg.

The rivers and lakes have played major roles in the settlement and development of the region. Early settlers took advantage of the easy water routes westward via the Ohio, the Great Lakes, and the Missouri; and commerce developed between the upper Mississippi and Ohio rivers and the Gulf Coast during the steamboat days that preceded the railroads in the first half of the nineteenth century. Today, the rivers are again undergoing rapid growth as carriers of commerce, and the fortuitous location of the Great Lakes Waterway between the rich iron-ore deposits of the Lake Superior Region and the coal deposits of the Appalachians has figured largely in the rapid growth of industry in the eastern United States. With the completion of the St. Lawrence Seaway, the Great Lakes cities have now become ports of call for oceangoing vessels from many nations.

THE PHYSIOGRAPHIC PROVINCES

On the basis of topography and geology the North Central States have been divided into a number of physiographic provinces. The most widely recognized divisions are those proposed by Fenneman (Figure 1).[1] These are the Appalachian Plateaus, the Central Lowland, the Interior Low Plateaus, the Ozark Plateaus, the Superior Uplands, and the Great Plains. None of these provinces is completely contained within the area of the North Central States.

The Appalachian Plateaus. This province is represented in the North Central States only in eastern Ohio, where it is a section of the subdivision referred to as the Allegheny Plateau. In northeastern Ohio, just south of Lake Erie, the Plateau is glaciated, but in southeastern Ohio only the western margin was invaded by glacial ice. The term "plateau" for this area is used primarily in the geological sense of an area of relatively horizontal sedimentary rocks standing above surrounding areas. Actually, much of it is highly dissected hill land of rather rugged relief. The sedimentary rocks in this province are primarily shales, sandstones, and conglomerates; and in eastern Ohio the Appalachian coal measures are represented, and some petroleum is produced. In the Ohio section of the Allegheny Plateau altitudes are moderate, averaging 1,200 to 1,400 feet above sealevel.

The Central Lowland. In many respects this province can be considered the real core of the North Central States. With a total area of approximately 444,000 square miles within the North Central States, this province contains about 45 percent of the total area of the region. Here, the combination of low relief, favorable climate, and good soils makes it one of the world's leading agricultural regions. Also, here are located vast resources of coal, moderate amounts of petroleum, and large quantities of building materials. It is the most industrialized and most densely populated province of the North Central States.

[1] Fenneman, Nevin M., *Physiography of the Western United States,* McGraw-Hill, New York, 1931; and *Physiography of the Eastern United States,* McGraw-Hill, New York, 1938.

Although the topography is subdued, the province contains a variety of relief types within its boundaries. Elevations range from less than 300 feet at the southern tip of Illinois to 1,500 feet along the western margin where it borders the Great Plains. On the east it is bounded by the higher, more rugged land of the Allegheny Plateau. In the northeast it extends beyond Lake Erie into southern Ontario where it meets the crystalline rocks of the Laurentian Upland, or what is commonly called the Canadian Shield. In northern Wisconsin and northeastern Minnesota it borders the Superior Upland, a southward extension of the Canadian Shield. To the south the Central Lowland is bounded by the Ozark Plateau Province in southern Missouri and by the Interior Low Plateaus Province in southern Illinois and southern Indiana. Along the southern boundary of Ohio it is terminated by the Ohio River. In many places this southern boundary is difficult to identify since usually it is considered to be the southern limit of glaciation. Where the glacial deposits are thin and eroded, the Central Lowland passes almost imperceptibly into the Interior Low Plateaus.

The western limit of the Central Lowland, where it meets the Great Plains, is not so well-established. A number of boundaries have been suggested corresponding to topography, geology, rainfall, and the 97th and 100th meridians. Fenneman considered the boundary to be the east-facing escarpment which rises 300 to 400 feet above the Central Lowland in North Dakota. This escarpment becomes less distinct southward and all but disappears in Nebraska where the 1,500-foot contour is used. In southern Kansas the boundary is again sharp where the Red Hills form a pronounced southeastward-facing escarpment 300 to 400 feet high.

The Central Lowland was the scene of the most widespread continental glaciation in the United States. With two exceptions, the whole of the area was covered by one or more of the continental glaciers during the Pleistocene Epoch of geologic time. Because of the significance to landscape, potential agricultural productivity, and land use, it is advantageous to divide the glaciated areas into the Old Drift Plains of Kansan and Illinoian age, and the Young Drift Plains of Wisconsin age. As will be demonstrated later, this distinction between Young Drift and Old Drift is an important one from the standpoint of soils and agriculture.

Two areas within the Central Lowland show little or no effects of glaciation. One is the famous Driftless Area, some 20,000 square miles in extent, centered in southwestern Wisconsin and extending into neighboring states. The Driftless Area stands in contrast to the subdued landscape adjacent to it, consisting of a dissected hill land resembling the Interior Low Plateaus. Recently, geologists have raised doubts about the term "driftless" for this area, but from a topographic standpoint, glacial influence on the topography is minimal. The other unglaciated area is the Osage Plains subdivision in west-central Missouri and southeastern Kansas, which extends beyond the boundaries of the North Central States into Oklahoma and Texas. The area can be described as a scarped plain with some escarpments rising as high as 600 feet above the intervening plains. A section of special interest because of the unique land use is the Flint Hills of eastern Kansas, where extensive natural prairie grasslands are utilized for grazing.

The Interior Low Plateaus. Only a small part of this province extends north of the Ohio River into Illinois and Indiana, where it merges with the Central Lowlands along the outer limits of continental glaciation. Unlike the glaciated areas to the north, bedrock structure and lithology control the topography; and in some areas such as southern Illinois, southwestern Indiana, and western Kentucky, faulting has played a major role, and intrusive volcanic rocks are associated with the faults. Important deposits of fluorspar (fluorite) are found in association with some of these fault zones in southern Illinois and western Kentucky. The rocks are mostly Paleozoic limestones, shales, and sandstones. Much of the area in southern Illinois and southern Indiana has a rugged, hilly topography with some areas of extensive lowlands, particularly along the

Mississippi and Wabash rivers. Loess caps most of the uplands, reaching its greatest thickness eastward from the major drainage ways.

Agriculturally, this area stands in contrast to the Central Lowland because of the limited amount of level land and less fertile soils. In many respects the area is economically and culturally transitional to the South.

The Ozark Plateau Province. This province covers an area of 40,000 square miles, about three-fourths of which lies within the North Central States in southern Missouri and southwestern Illinois. In western Missouri is a subdivision known as the Springfield Plateau, where extensive level interfluves separate valleys cut 200 to 300 feet below the upland surface. In some areas hills of resistant rock reach elevations of 1,000 to 1,500 feet above sea level, and the area is mantled by chert which has weathered from the limestone bedrock. The major subdivision of the province is the Salem Plateau which extends eastward across southern Missouri and across the Mississippi River into Illinois. The Salem Plateau consists primarily of limestones and dolomites. Local relief on the dissected interfluves between the major streams rarely exceeds 100 feet, but may be as much as 500 feet adjacent to the large stream valleys such as the White and Gasconade rivers. Much of the area is in steep slopes but numerous upland flats exist, justifying the term "plateau" rather than "hill lands." A conspicuous characteristic of the area is the presence of numerous large springs, which place Missouri second only to Idaho in the number of springs exceeding 100 cubic feet per second flow.

The St. Francois Mountains of southeastern Missouri are unique in geology and topography for the east-central United States. Here, ancient Precambrian rocks have been exhumed by erosion of the Ozark dome, and the area presents a topography characterized by bold igneous hills, which contrasts with the typical Ozark topography formed by the dissection of sedimentary rocks. One of these granite peaks, Tom Sauk Mountain, reaches an elevation of 1,700 feet, the highest point in Missouri. In the igneous rocks of the area and along the contacts with the sedimentary rocks are found valuable deposits of lead and iron ore.

Like the Interior Low Plateaus, this area presents a sharp contrast to a major part of the North Central States. Here, agriculture is severely limited by topography and soils, much of the land is in forests, and the way of life has much in common with that of the Appalachians.

The rough terrain and numerous streams with a reputation for sport fishing have proved to be tourist attractions. Added to the natural attractions have been a number of artificial lakes which draw thousands into the area for boating and water sports. Although not as well-developed as in some other tourist areas, tourism holds considerable promise for future growth.

The Great Plains Province. This is the second most extensive physiographic province of the North Central States, containing about 40 percent of the total area. This area is a part of the physiographic province which extends without interruption from the Mexican border northward into the Prairie Provinces of Canada. To the east it is bounded by the Central Lowland and to the west by the Rocky Mountains. Elevations range from about 1,500 feet on the east to over 5,000 feet in the west. The province contains numerous outliers of the Rocky Mountains, typical of which is the Black Hills subdivision, where elevations reach 7,742 feet in Harney Peak. Although most areas show little local relief, there are some areas where topographic expression lends variety to the landscape. Geologically, the province differs from the eastern part of the North Central States in that the sedimentary rocks are generally younger, being chiefly Mesozoic and Cenezoic in age in contrast to the preponderance of Paleozoic rocks to the east.

On the basis of topography several subdivisions of the Great Plains may be recognized within the North Central States. On the north in Montana, North Dakota, South Dakota, and northeastern Wyoming is the Missouri Plateau. This subdivision is divided into the glaciated section, usually called the *Coteau du Missouri,* to the east of the Missouri River, and the unglaciated section to the west. Both of these subdivisions contain outliers of the Rocky Mountains.

Surrounded by the Missouri Plateau is the Black Hills subdivision, which is the major eastern outlier of the Rocky Mountains and consists of an eroded dome in which the core of Precambrian crystalline rock is exposed. The High Plains section is bounded on the north by the north-facing Pine Ridge Escarpment, which locally rises 1,000 feet above the Missouri Plateau. In many areas the High Plains section is capped with a veneer of Tertiary and Pleistocene sediments that have been carried out from the base of the Rocky Mountains, and the landscape is prevailingly one of deposition rather than erosion. This subdivision is located chiefly in Nebraska, southeastern Wyoming, eastern Colorado, and western Kansas. An important area within the High Plains subdivision is the Sand Hills region of western Nebraska, an area of 24,000 square miles where stabilized, grass-covered sand dunes dominate the landscape.

Adjacent to the Rocky Mountain front in Colorado is the Colorado Piedmont subdivision, an area where erosion has removed the younger sediments causing it to be lower in elevation than the High Plains to the east. South of the Colorado Piedmont, in southern Colorado and northeastern New Mexico, is the Raton section, where high lava-capped mesas and other volcanic features are found. The remaining subdivision of the Great Plains, the Plains Border section, lies mostly in central Kansas and is a broad area of dissected topography along the eastern margin of the Plains, where the younger sediments are being eroded back from the Central Lowland, exposing older sediments to the east.

From the standpoint of agriculture, population, and regional economy, the Great Plains Province offers another area of contrast to the Central Lowland. Here, rainfall is the limiting factor, resulting in extensive cultivation of cash grains and grazing of natural-grass rangelands. Population density falls off rapidly westward, where most areas have fewer than 18 persons per square mile, and in some areas the density falls below five. Only along the Colorado Piedmont where agriculture is more intense under irrigation and where industry has developed, do population densities again reach those of the western part of the Central Lowland.

The Superior Upland. This region, like the other bordering areas of the North Central States, varies considerably in its physical characteristics from the Central Lowland. It occupies the northern part of Wisconsin, northeastern Minnesota, and most of the Upper Peninsula of Michigan. The sedimentary rocks of the Central Lowland give way to the complex Precambrian rocks which extend southward from the Canadian Shield. Because of glaciation and the thickness of the glacial deposits, it is often difficult to locate the exact boundaries of the province on the basis of its bedrock geology, particularly in Minnesota.

The area abounds in lakes of glacial origin. In the south, these lakes lie in depressions in the glacial sediments, while in the north they occupy rock basins scoured out by the advancing ice. The geologic structure of the area is extremely complex, and many types of old sedimentary, igneous, and metamorphic rocks abound. Many hills rise several hundred feet above the general level of the Superior Upland, and a few reach elevations just under 2,000 feet above sea level.

Much of the area is forested, and forest products are important in the regional economy. Agricultural potential is limited by topography and soils. It is an area of outstanding mineral resources, particularly iron-ore deposits, which are the most productive in the United States. Also, important copper deposits are mined in Michigan on the Keweenaw Peninsula on the south shore of Lake Superior.

Although glaciation left a legacy of poor soils and limited agricultural opportunities, it provided the area with great potential for recreation. The vast number of lakes set in the forest environment provide excellent fishing and opportunities for boating, canoeing, and water sports. With the large metropolitan centers of the Lower Great Lakes within a relatively short distance by highway, the province is proving increasingly attractive for vacations. Winter sports are developing to help make the tourist industry a year-round business. Because of the limited potential for development along other lines of economic endeavor, tourism seems destined to become the major industry for the Superior Uplands outside the mining communities.

CLIMATE

Because of the absence of major topographic barriers and the lack of abrupt changes in elevation of sufficient magnitude to be of climatic significance, the climates of the North Central States merge with one another along zones of transition. The boundaries that appear on a map of climatic subdivisions are, in reality, statistically derived lines based on years of climatic records, and therefore shift from year to year with variations in temperature and precipitation. Generally speaking, rainfall declines from east to west across the area, and temperature and length of growing season decrease from south to north. It is variations in these climatic factors that give the region's considerable climatic diversity.

Of all the factors of the physical environment, climate is of paramount importance to agriculture. Precipitation and temperature, in large part, determine the suitability of an area for given crops. Even where irrigation is practiced, the sources of water are ultimately controlled by climate. Because of man's inability to control the weather or predict what it will be for any extended period of time, a considerable element of chance is introduced into agriculture. One year may produce bumper crops when the weather is favorable, and crop failure when it is not. However, long observations of the fluctuations in weather have made it possible to adapt agricultural activities to conform to some degree with the patterns of climate.

Precipitation. In the southeastern part of the North Central States average annual precipitation in equivalent inches of rainfall is in excess of 45 inches in southeastern Missouri and southern Indiana, and much of the Ohio River valley receives in excess of 40 inches (Figure 2). Westward, annual precipitation declines to about 20 inches at the western margin of the Central Lowland and to less than 15 inches on the western Great Plains.

On the basis of average annual precipitation, the area can be divided into the humid east and the dry west. The line of division is not far from the topographic division between the Central Lowland and the Great Plains and is, in fact, sometimes used to mark the boundary between these two provinces. In the north an average annual rainfall of 20 inches is sufficient to make the area humid, but in the south the division between humid and dry is closer to the 30-inch average rainfall line. This boundary between humid and dry climates follows a north-south line from northwestern Minnesota through southeastern South Dakota, eastern Nebraska, and eastern Kansas.

Seasonal distribution of precipitation is a major factor in agriculture. Although total annual precipitation decreases toward the west, the warm-season precipitation (April through September) tends to increase slightly while cool-season precipitation decreases, resulting in an increasing concentration during the growing season. For example, in southern Ohio 55 percent of the average rainfall comes in the growing season, while in Iowa over 70 percent falls in that part of the year (Table 1).

Fluctuations in precipitation from year to year also have significant effect on crop yields. Annual totals are often misleading since dry spells at critical times in the development of a crop may result in reduced yields even though the annual total is normal or even above normal. In the same sense, too much rain in critical periods

TABLE 1

Selected Climatic Stations in the North Central States

Station	Climatic Type *	Average Temperature Jan. (°F.)	July (°F.)	Growing Season (average days)	Average Annual Precip. (inches)	% of Average Precipitation April–Sept.
Cairo, Ill.	Humid Subtropical	36.8	79.7	217	40.46	49
Urbana, Ill.	Humid Continental (Warm Summer)	26.7	75.5	180	35.54	60
Columbus, Ohio	Humid Continental (Warm Summer)	30.5	75.4	187	34.10	54
Duluth, Minn.	Humid Continental (Cool Summer)	9.1	64.9	148	26.51	69
Itaska State Park, Minn.	Humid Continental (Cool Summer)	3.3	66.8	99	22.68	75
Bismarck, N.D.	Midlatitude Steppe	9.4	70.9	140	15.43	77
Denver, Colorado	Midlatitude Steppe	32.0	72.5	171	13.99	62
Garden City, Kan.	Midlatitude Steppe	30.9	72.5	174	18.88	75

* Based on Trewartha's modification of Köppen.
Source: U.S. Department of Agriculture, *Climate and Man*, 1941 Yearbook of Agriculture.

may reduce yields. Drought years also occur with the probability of severe drought increasing from east to west. Exceptionally damaging and widespread droughts have affected the North Central States during a number of years since modern settlement of the area, the most recent being the very severe droughts of the early and mid-1930's and the mid-1950's. During the worst drought years the western part of the North Central States had arid to semiarid climates, while the remainder was subhumid. Fortunately, severe droughts tend to be localized and only during exceptional years like 1934 and 1936 have they affected almost all of the North Central States simultaneously.

Temperature. Great contrast between winter and summer and rapid changes from day to day characterize the temperature regime of the North Central States. This has been well-illustrated during the few days in mid-January while this chapter is being written in Des Moines, Iowa. On this Tuesday morning the temperature stands at 12° F. Last Saturday, after a long spell of unseasonably warm weather with highs in the upper 40's, the temperature dropped to —12° F. in the space of a few hours. However, by Sunday afternoon it was again in the mid-40's and then again down to +12° F. by Monday morning.

These marked fluctuations in temperature are characteristic in varying degree of all portions of the midcontinent, where no climatically significant topographic barriers exist between the Arctic Ocean and the Gulf of Mexico. This makes it possible for air with polar characteristics to flow in on one side of cyclonic storms and tropical air on the other, thereby causing air masses of radically different temperature characteristics to alternate frequently in their dominance of the area. Adding to the effect is the continental location. Within the continental interior of North America, the moderating effects of the oceans are minimized, and the rapid response of the land mass to seasonal changes in solar radiation is reflected in the extremes between winter and summer.

A comparison of temperatures from north to south across the central United States will show that the temperature gradient is much steeper in winter. For example, the average July temperature at Des Moines is 76° F. while at New Orleans it is 80° F., a difference of only 4°. However, the January average at Des Moines is about 21° F. while that of New Orleans is 53° F., a difference of 32°.

Extremes of temperature between winter and summer are characteristic of the midcontinent. All of the area except that in the vicinity of the south shore of Lake Superior and a part of the east shore of Lake Michigan has experienced temperatures above 100° F. during the period for which records have been kept. A few areas have recorded temperatures above 115° F., mostly during the dry years of the mid-1930's. Extremely low temperatures in winter have fallen below —50° F. in some locations, and almost all areas have observed readings below —20° F.

The long-term view of temperature is perhaps best illustrated by the length of the growing season, which is the average number of consecutive days without a killing frost. Since the practical limits of various crops are determined by the growing season, it is of particularly great importance to agriculture. The average length of the frost-free period in the North Central States ranges from more than 200 days in extreme southern Illinois and southeastern Missouri, to less than 100 days in some areas of northern Minnesota. Most of the area falls within the range of 120 to 180 days (Table 1).

Climatic Types. According to the Trewartha modification of the Köppen classification of climates, the southern margin of the North Central States is Humid Subtropical with mild winters and hot, humid summers. In the extreme southern part of Illinois and southeastern Missouri, the growing season exceeds 210 days, and cotton becomes practicable as a cash crop. This climatic type is also found in southern Kansas, Indiana, and Ohio.

Northward from the Humid Subtropical climatic area is the long-summer or warm-summer phase of Humid Continental climate with hot summers and cold winters. This climate area closely approximates the agricultural heart of the area, the Corn Belt. Growing seasons average well over 100 days in most areas, and exceed 180 days in the south. The cool-summer phase of Humid Continental climate characterizes the northern border states from the eastern Dakotas through the Great Lakes area. Here, the winters are very severe, and, in many areas, the growing season averages less than 100 days.

West of the humid climates is the dry Midlatitude Steppe climate area, which corresponds with most of the Great Plains area. Rainfall is everywhere less than 20 inches, and droughts are a frequent menace to agriculture. In the more favored areas, grain farming, particularly wheat, is possible through dry-farming methods; while toward the drier margins, livestock ranching and irrigated agriculture represent an adjustment to the dry climate.

Climate and Man. Besides having effects on agriculture, climate plays an important role in the day-to-day lives of the people of the North Central States. The continental climate of most of the area requires special adjustments in housing, clothing, and transportation, which the Midwesterner takes as a matter of course. Houses must be insulated against the cold winters, and, in recent decades, air conditioning has helped alleviate the unpleasantness of the hot, humid summers. In the last few years public utility companies have reported that summer has now become the peak season for power demand in much of the Midwest because of air conditioning in homes, offices, and places of business.

Winter's heavy snow necessitates the expenditure of large sums of money for snow and ice removal from highways and streets. Heating is expensive for both home owners and business men, and furnishes a growing market for natural gas from the midcontinent fields. Farmers must have well-constructed barns and shelters for livestock, and blizzards may result in great loss of cattle on the

Great Plains. On the credit side the severe winters encourage the development of commercial winter sports areas, particularly in the Upper Great Lakes region where snowfall is very heavy and snow cover is prolonged.

Violent and changeable weather is the lot of the heart of the continent. In addition to the violent blizzards that often follow in the wake of arctic air invasions from Canada, there are the violent thunderstorms of spring and summer. Often these thunderstorms harbor tornadoes, the most destructive of weather phenomena, and hail, which may lay waste to crops. To designate the climate of the North Central States as "temperate" is certainly a misnomer.

NATURAL VEGETATION

The vegetation cover of the area, as observed by the first settlers from the east, reflected in a general way the climatic pattern. The approximate distribution of natural vegetation at the time of settlement is shown in Figure 3. In the humid eastern portion broadleaf deciduous forests dominated by oak and hickory were the rule. In the Great Lakes region northern coniferous forests and mixed coniferous-deciduous forests reflected the transition to the boreal forests (taiga) of the Canadian Subarctic. Toward the drier west, grasslands replaced trees on the Great Plains and in the prairie wedge which extended eastward into Iowa, northern Missouri, southern Minnesota, northern Illinois, and northwestern Indiana. This wedge-shaped area of tall-grass prairie presents somewhat of a vegetation anomaly in the humid east, since present climate seems well-suited to trees. A number of theories have been advanced to explain the prairies of the North Central States, including the role of fire in maintaining this biome against invasion by trees.

The impact of modern agriculture on the natural vegetation has destroyed forest and grassland alike, replacing the natural vegetation cover by what has been termed a "cultural steppe" dominated by cultivated crops, particularly corn, small grains, and forage. Perhaps no natural biome has been so thoroughly eradicated by man as has that of the North American prairies, where level land and adequate precipitation resulted in a high percentage of the surface being put to the plow. Today, sizable remnants of the oak-hickory forest remain in the rougher areas, but one must search diligently along railroad rights-of-way and in the few poorly drained areas to find the prairie in something of its original state. One exception is the Flint Hills of eastern Kansas, where extensive areas of natural tall-grass prairies are preserved in commercial grazing lands.

The short-grass steppes of the Great Plains also have felt the eradicating impact of the plow, but in the drier areas and in areas such as the Nebraska Sand Hills, large expanses remain as grazing lands. Here, cattle have replaced the bison, and overgrazing undoubtedly has altered somewhat the relative abundance of vegetation forms.

The northern forests of the Great Lakes region have been extensively exploited for lumber and pulp, and large parts of the cut-over area are now covered with weed trees of little value except for deer browse. However, in some areas not well-suited to cultivation, the forest has survived the period of destructive exploitation and contributes to the support of an important forest-products industry.

SOILS

In an area so important to the agricultural base of the United States, soils form an important natural resource. Although considerable areas have limited soil resources, larger areas have excellent soils which rank among the world's finest. Although hundreds of soil types can be found within any given region, they can be broadly classified into great soil groups that conform closely to the climatic and vegetation zones.[2]

[2] In 1960, the Soil Conservation Service adopted a new soil classification system to replace the Great Soil Groups. However, the old system seems more appropriate for a brief description of the soils as here given. For a summary of the new system see: U.S. Department of Agriculture, *Soil Classification, a Comprehensive System, 7th Approximation,* Soil Survey Staff, Soil Conservation Service, 1960.

In the humid east the soils which developed under the broad-leaf deciduous forests belong to the great soil group called the *gray-brown podzolic*. These soils are acid and of moderate fertility. With the addition of lime and fertilizers and under proper management practices they have been made highly productive for crops such as corn and small grains. The best of the gray-brown podzolic soils are developed on the young glacial drifts of Wisconsin age. Artificial drainage has been necessary on many of these young glacial soils to make them suitable for agriculture. Today, these soils are second in productivity only to the young glacial soils of the prairie grasslands to the west.

The prairie soils or *brunizems* are the most productive of the great soil groups in the North Central States. Although they are mildly acid due to the leaching of carbonates under the humid climate, they are rich in organic matter and high in nitrogen. From a fertility standpoint, they are not as rich as some of the dry grassland soils to the west; but because of more abundant precipitation, they yield higher returns to agriculture. The parent material of these soils is glacial drift or loess and many areas require artificial drainage by ditch and tile. On the younger drift plains of southern Minnesota, northern Iowa, and northern Illinois, over 25 percent of the area is level to nearly level and over half of the land is in corn.

The soils of the dry grasslands are less subjected to leaching of soluble minerals and therefore are high in lime and nitrogen. West of a line from extreme northwestern Minnesota, south through eastern Nebraska and central Kansas, the soils are basic; and the addition of lime, so necessary east of this line, is not so important. The *chernozems,* located along the eastern margins of the short-grass steppes are the best of the dry grassland soils. They are high in organic material, which gives them a dark-brown to black color, and are rich in plant nutrients. These are probably the best wheat soils and are similar to soils of this group in the steppes of the Soviet Union. However, yields from agriculture on these soils are lower than on the less-fertile prairie soils to the east because of the lower and less reliable rainfall. As rainfall diminishes westward across the Great Plains, the chernozems give way to the chestnut soils and eventually to the brown soils. On these soils some agriculture is practiced through dry farming, but risk from drought is high. Where irrigation water is not available, large areas of these soils are used for grazing.

North of the gray-brown podzolic soils and the prairie soils, in the area of the northern forests, are soils belonging to the zonal type called *podzols*. These soils are the product of cool, moist climates and coniferous forests. They are generally light colored, acid, low in organic matter, and relatively infertile. Because of glaciation and poor drainage, bog soils occupy millions of acres. Poor soils and relatively good soils are intermingled, and a single farm rarely has a high percentage of good land. The average farm in this area has less than 40 acres of cropland, and the pastured woodland often exceeds cultivated acreage. Much of the land, especially if poorly drained, remains in forests.

South of the prairie soils of Illinois and Iowa are soils formed on broad, flat uplands where claypans have formed, reducing their agricultural capacity. These soils are called *planosols* and have formed on fine-textured loess over old glacial drifts under grass or deciduous forests. Farther to the south, in the Ozark uplands of southern Missouri and the hills of southern Illinois, the soils belong to the group called red and yellow soils. They are highly leached, low in organic matter, and of limited fertility. These red and yellow soils are characteristic of areas of the southeastern United States where the climate is Humid Subtropical.

All of these soil regions contain azonal and intrazonal soils that do not fit into the zonal classification. Chief among these are the bog soils, half-bog soils (*wisenboden*), shallow stony soils (*lithosols*), sands, and alluvial soils, in addition to the panosols already mentioned.

MAN AND THE PHYSICAL SETTING

In retrospect, the physical environment and the resource base of the North Central States have played a major role in the successful development of this area into an outstanding agricultural and manufacturing region among the world's regions. However, to the first explorers of European origin it must have seemed, in many ways, a formidable area to conquer. The great forests offered game, furs for trade, and raw materials for homes, and were assumed to be potentially fertile lands for agricultural settlement. The vast grasslands were beyond the experience of most Europeans and were considered a hostile environment with little potential for settlement. Beyond the Mississippi and Missouri rivers early maps indicated the Great American Desert in areas that today have a productive agriculture.

Indian settlement in the area may date to the waning days of the last glacial period, and radiocarbon dates of over 10,000 years ago have been reported for prehistoric settlements along the western margins of the Great Plains. Early agriculturalists introduced corn or maize into the region as a vital part of their neolithic farming, a crop destined to revolutionize North American agriculture. These early hunters and farmers may have contributed to the survival and expansion of the humid prairies by the use of fire; but even the Indian was not completely at home on the Great Plains until the European horse was adopted, and the recent Plains Indian culture flowered in time to meet American expansion head-on in the later half of the nineteenth century.

The expansion of the American nation into this heartland of the continent is one of the great epics of modern times. Beginning with the preliminary assault on the unknown by Spanish, French, English, and, later, American explorers, trappers, and traders, and followed by the permanent settlers' pushing the frontier westward, the conquest of the area now comprising the North Central States was not complete until the closing decades of the nineteenth century. The account of this westward expansion, the subsequent establishment of the present pattern of settlement, and the utilization and development of the resource base, all have a major bearing on the present character of the region.

The following chapters will consider the ways in which modern man has adapted his agricultural activities to the diverse environments of the North Central States, and how he has exploited forests and mineral deposits to lay the foundations for a modern industrial society. Often this exploitation has been destructive with little thought for future generations; but with a maturing of our society, a more rational approach to resource use seems to be developing.

2 The Settlement of the North Central States

MUCH could be written about the explorers, hunters, traders, and the historic and prehistoric Indian inhabitants of the area that now comprises the North Central States. However, we are concerned here with the westward movement of permanent settlement, which, after a century-and-a-half of confinement east of the Appalachians, finally spilled westward and in less than a century occupied most of the continent.

The treaty with England which ended the American Revolution in 1783 recognized the new nation's claim to the area west of the Appalachians, north of the Ohio River, and west to the Mississippi. The first step in opening up this vast territory to orderly settlement was the agreement of the eastern seaboard states to grant concessions to the Federal Government of their claims to the lands in the west. In the area north of the Ohio River and east of the Mississippi River, the chief concessions were made by Virginia, New York, Massachusetts, and Connecticut. With control of the lands of the west in the hands of the United States Government, the problem of how to dispose of the public domain and encourage settlement was paramount.

Two systems for disposal of new lands were already established on the eastern seaboard: that of surveying lands in orderly blocks before selling them to settlers, a system characteristic of New England, or the southern practice of indiscriminate location of settle-

31

ments and subsequent survey. The advantage of the first was that westward advancement in compact tiers was assured, but poor land had to be purchased along with the good. The southern system permitted the selection of only the good land, but this often led to conflicting claims and irregularly shaped plots which were difficult to survey.

The problem was resolved by the Ordinance of 1785, one of the most fundamental legislative measures in the history of the United States. This ordinance established the Township and Range system of land survey, which has left its imprint on settlement patterns, land ownership, and road systems in a large part of the area west of the Appalachians. This ordinance also provided for dividing all government-owned land into townships six miles square. These, in turn, were subdivided into 36 equal sections numbered systematically from 1 through 36, each theoretically one mile square or 640 acres.[1] A systematic system of numbering the townships, principal meridians and base lines, and the sections within the townships made it possible to identify and locate any surveyed parcels of land and allowed them to be sold at auction in the east, often sight-unseen. Provisions were made to allot rights-of-way for public roads for each square section, and one section in each township was set aside for maintenance of schools.

The striking rectangular pattern of fields, roads, and even towns and cities in the central and western United States owes its existence to the land survey rules laid down in the Ordinance of 1785. The provisions for purchasing land by sections and square parcels within sections assured a dispersed rural population and prevented develop-

[1] In actual practice the sections are not always exactly one mile square. Since the townships are bounded by north-south lines (meridians) which converge toward the poles, it was necessary to correct the survey along correction lines at intervals to compensate for this convergence. Therefore, some sections near the correction lines have considerably fewer acres than 640. The details of this survey system are outlined in most introductory physical geography or cartography texts.

ment of agricultural villages, which are the rule throughout most of the world's agricultural regions.[2]

PIONEER SETTLEMENT OF THE HUMID EAST

Response to the opening of the lands in the west was immediate. After more than a century of being blocked from westward expansion by the French and Indian barrier, the eastern seaboard was becoming overcrowded, and the western frontier beckoned those whose economic plight was not good in the east. It also brought land speculators and adventurers, but the land was settled so rapidly that by the end of the first half of the nineteenth century the frontier extended well beyond the Mississippi River into Iowa and Missouri (Figure 4).

Small-scale movements of people from the eastern seaboard to the lands west of the Appalachians had begun in the mid-eighteenth century. By the time of the Revolution, scattered settlement had pushed westward from the forks of the Ohio River into the Kentucky bluegrass region and the valley of the Tennessee River. In the decade following the Revolution, Kentucky and Tennessee filled rapidly with settlers, and in 1792 Kentucky was admitted to statehood, followed four years later by Tennessee. The course of settlement then shifted northward across the Ohio with Kentucky and Tennessee furnishing a large share of the settlers to what was to become Ohio, Indiana, and Illinois. In the Land Act of 1800, Ohio was split off from the remainder of the Old Northwest, and it became a state in 1803.

Between 1800 and the War of 1812, Ohio received settlers from New England, the Middle Atlantic States, and the South. Even the

[2] The striking pattern, on aerial photographs, produced on the land by various systems of land division in the United States can be seen in the excellent publication, *Land Use and its Patterns in the United States,* Agricultural Handbook No. 153, U.S. Department of Agriculture, Superintendent of Documents, Washington, D.C., 1959.

populations of whole villages were transplanted to Ohio soil, where replicas were created of the villages that had been left behind in New Engand. By 1812, the population of the state had exceeded 250,000, and the area began to resemble the eastern seaboard rather than the frontier.

Prior to 1812, the Michigan Territory, the Indiana Territory, and the Illinois Territory had been set aside. The Michigan Territory remained relatively unsettled until after the War of 1812, while Indiana had grown to a population of about 25,000 and Illinois to 13,000 before the war called a temporary halt to the westward movement of settlement.

At the close of the War of 1812, the major part of the population of the North Central States was confined to the eastern and southern parts of Ohio and to a narrow band along the Ohio River westward to its junction with the Mississippi. Between 1815 and 1830 settlement progressed rapidly in the forested areas south of the prairies in Indiana and Illinois, with the southern uplands supplying most of the immigrants. Many came by way of the Cumberland Gap in eastern Tennessee, while others used the National Road, which stretched from Baltimore to Wheeling and was later extended westward to Columbus. Others came down the Ohio River to Shawneetown in the Illinois Territory and across southern Illinois to the Mississippi River towns of Kaskaskia, Cahokia, St. Louis, and Alton. Particularly attractive to farmers were the rich American Bottoms, which stretched along the east bank of the Mississippi below the mouth of the Missouri. Other bottomlands such as those of the Wabash and other rivers were favored spots for settlement in the hilly lands bordering the Ohio and Mississippi rivers. Most settlers avoided the prairies because of lack of techniques and tools for cultivating the deep, heavy sod and because of the unfounded prejudice that land without trees was not fertile. Indiana was admitted to statehood in 1816 and Illinois in 1818.

During the early period (1815–1830), settlement also spread into the Driftless Area of southwestern Wisconsin, northeastern Iowa, and northwestern Illinois in response to the developing lead mining of the district. Galena was founded as the center of the mining district, from which around 15 million pounds of lead were sent annually down the Mississippi to New Orleans. Settlers had also pushed westward across the Mississippi and along the Missouri River after the Louisiana Purchase of 1803, and Missouri was admitted to statehood in 1821.

After the opening of the Erie Canal to traffic in 1825, the stream of immigration was deflected from the Ohio Valley to the Great Lakes, and Michigan attained statehood in 1837. Many of the immigrants to northern Indiana, northern Illinois, and southern Michigan came from New England, where economic conditions were unsettled as the result of the early stages of the industrial revolution. Later, increased competition of cheap grains from west of the Appalachians forced many farmers in New England and other east-coast areas to give up and move westward.

At first, settlement stopped at the edge of the prairies in northern Illinois; but as land became more scarce, later settlers pushed onto the prairies. With the development of new techniques to break the heavy sod it soon became apparent that the cost of sod-breaking could be paid for with a few good crops. The good yields from the deep prairie soils soon laid to rest the old fallacy that prairies were not fertile. By 1850, almost the entire state of Illinois was settled, and the frontier of settlement had moved northward into southern Wisconsin and westward into eastern and southern Iowa. In 1846, Iowa attained statehood, followed two years later by Wisconsin.

During the 1850's the eastern margins of Nebraska and Kansas and the southeastern part of Minnesota were occupied, chiefly by settlers from the adjacent states to the east. Minnesota was admitted to the Union in 1857. Kansas became the scene of conflict between the pro-slavery forces and the abolitionists, and the resulting unsettled conditions discouraged many potential settlers from moving into the territory. During the Civil War, Kansas and Nebraska remained strongly pro-Union and were rewarded with statehood during and shortly after the war, Kansas in 1861 and Nebraska in 1867. Thus, by the close of the Civil War, a major part of the humid eastern section of the North Central States had been settled, and future westward movement faced a new environment, the dry Great Plains.

THE SETTLEMENT OF THE GREAT PLAINS

Although the Great Plains had been repeatedly crossed by western migrants to the mountain areas and the California gold fields and by the fur traders, permanent settlement was delayed until after the Civil War. In the first two decades after the war the settlement of the plains was by cattlemen, while farmers paused at the eastern margin of this unfamiliar environment. Cattle-ranching was ideally suited to the grasslands, and growing eastern markets promised an outlet for beef and, eventually, wool. Farmers had to wait until the 1870's, when technology in farm equipment and methods made cultivation of the dry plains a possibility.

The Open Range. The two decades during which the cattlemen dominated the Great Plains is one of the most picturesque periods of American history, as is evidenced by the legends of the era, which are kept alive in perverted form by western movies and the TV western. In the initial stages great herds of longhorns were driven northward from Texas to the railheads at Abilene and Dodge City for sale to cattle buyers for export to eastern markets. These longhorn cattle were derived from herds grazed on open ranges by Mexican cattlemen who perfected the open-range system. The cattle were long, rangy *ganado criollo,* whose ancestors were Moorish cattle brought from Spain to the New World colonies. They were well-adapted to conditions of the Great Plains, but were less well-suited for market. Later, they were crossed with other cattle from the eastern states to produce animals more to the liking of eastern buyers. Eventually, Hereford bulls were brought in for breeding, and the predominant "white faced" cattle became the trademark of the western range.

Although picturesque and the subject of legend and song, the long overland cattle drives were economically unsound. Losses were high and the surviving cattle lost much weight. Farmers objected to the destructive herds as did the Indians in Oklahoma Territory whose lands had to be crossed. It soon became obvious that the solution to profitable cattle-ranching was to move the operation nearer the railroads. Thus, the cattle industry shifted northward, and by the end of the 1860's cattle ranches were widespread in Kansas and Nebraska. In the 1870's railroads were pushed westward, and growing markets in the east assured sound profits for the successful ranchers. Ranching also spread westward with the railroad and eventually covered most of the plains. Because of the early attraction of gold mining, Colorado was settled earlier than the Plains States to the east, and gained statehood in 1876. By 1880, with the last of the great Indian wars over in the Dakota Territory, ranching had become well-established in the dry western area of the North Central States.

The open-range phase of the settlement of the Great Plains was short-lived. Falling prices and a series of climatic disasters, culminating in the disastrous winter of 1886–1887, ended the open-range phase of the cattle industry. Already, the farmer was pushing out onto the dry plains, and barbed wire fences were enclosing the range.

Agricultural Settlement of the Great Plains. During the first half of the nineteenth century, maps appeared with the legend "Great American Desert" spread across the area from the Rocky Mountains to western Nebraska and Kansas. This was based largely on reports of such explorers as Pike and Long, in which the drier western plains were compared with the sandy wastes of the Sahara, and on writings of armchair geographers and travelers. It was not until the mid-nineteenth century that a truer picture began to emerge from official railroad surveys, in which the High Plains were compared, with some validity, to the Russian steppes.

Early impressions of the climate of the Great Plains were, necessarily, the result of observations of the natural vegetation. The lack of trees and the dominance of grass led many observers to conclude that the steppes would never be suitable for cultivation and were destined to remain the province of the Indians, or at best, the cattlemen. Later, when scattered climatic records were obtained, a likewise erroneous impression of abundance of rainfall led to an overly optimistic evaluation of the agricultural potential. This was especially true since the first wave of agricultural settlement coincided with a period of above normal precipitation, thus seeming to substantiate the old fallacy that "rainfall follows the plow," only to have the belief exploded by disastrous droughts. We know from many years of observation that periods of above-average rainfall are followed by dry periods, the below-average years seeming to outnumber the wet years.

In spite of early pessimism and later overoptimism, the agricultural settlement of the Great Plains was inevitable. Land for settlement was becoming scarce in the humid east, the great flood of immigrants from northern Europe was supplying land-hungry settlers, and technology was supplying the tools and techniques for conquering the new environment for agriculture. The debate still goes on as to whether the grasslands should have been put to the plow; the opponents of cultivation of the plains can point to the disastrous droughts and dust-bowl conditions of the 1930's and, more recently, the mid-1950's. On the other hand, this area now constitutes one of the major agricultural regions of the United States for the production of grains for domestic and export markets. Without the agriculture of the Great Plains, American agriculture, and to some extent, world supplies of bread grains, would have assumed a different character.

Government Policies and Settlement. Government policies in the United States have traditionally favored agriculture and agricultural settlement. However, the stated purposes of these policies have not always been realized, as is well-illustrated in the record of land distribution in the Great Plains. During the latter half of the nineteenth century, several acts of Congress facilitated the settlement of the steppes by a farming population. Earliest of these was the Homestead Act of 1862. This act provided that for a fee of ten dollars any citizen, or alien who had filed for first citizenship papers, could lay claim to 160 acres of public domain and could receive final title after five years of residence and cultivation of the land. It is obvious now that the standard homestead of 160 acres failed to meet the needs for settlement of the dry lands west of the 98th meridian. Ranching required 2,000 or more acres, while extensive farming needed 360 to 640 acres to be profitable. On the other hand, irrigation farmers needed only 40 to 60 acres for an economically viable unit. The inadequacy of the provisions of the Homestead Act was stressed in Major John W. Powell's *Report on the Lands of the Arid Region of the United States*. Powell recommended a provision for homesteads of 2,560 acres of land, an amount that seemed ridiculously large to eastern Congressmen.

Later attempts to remedy the deficiencies of the Homestead Act were of little value to the individual settler, but deficiencies and loopholes were seized upon by land speculators and ranchers to enlarge their holdings. Also, the generous federal grants to railroads withheld millions of acres of the best land from the land-hungry farmers. Ultimately, the stated purpose of the Homestead Act and subsequent acts was circumvented with a major share of the public domain going to corporations, states, and particularly railroads. By 1887, only 600,000 homesteads were recorded by the Land Office, with a total of 80 million acres, about 17 percent of the total public domain which had been disposed of. Undoubtedly, many of these homesteads were fraudulent, obtained by ranchers and speculators through devious means. At the same time, railroads had received some 181 million acres and the states 140 million, while 100 million acres had been sold directly by the Land Office, chiefly to land speculators. Generally, the would-be homesteader was faced with the choice of isolated, substandard homesteads or purchase of land from land companies, speculators, or railroads at relatively high prices for the time.[3]

In spite of all of the obstacles of climate, failures of government plans to get land of the public domain into the hands of the landless, and economic crises, the western lands of the North Central States were settled by a permanent agricultural and ranching population. A glance at Figure 4, showing the westward march of the frontier, will give some indication of the periods during which settlement occurred. In 1889 North Dakota, South Dakota, and Montana became states, followed in 1890 by Wyoming. In the closing decade of the nineteenth century, the frontier period essentially came to an end.

Technology and the Agricultural Settlement of the Great Plains. In his book *Westward Expansion,* Ray Billington points out that the Great Plains could be utilized by adapting to the section's unique features as was done by the cattlemen during the open-range period, or by the application of products and techniques of the industrial revolution to conquer nature's obstacles. The real conquest was made possible by the inventors, laborers, and industrialists who applied the techniques of the industrial revolution to the problems inherent in the last major American frontier.[4]

Good fences were a primary requirement for farming on the plains. Roving range cattle would make short work of planted crops, and bitter arguments ensued between farmer and cattleman along the eastern margins of the Great Plains as to whose responsibility it was to fence the range. When wood was the only fencing material, cost of this imported material was prohibitive for the farmer, an estimated investment of about $1,000 being required to fence a 160-acre homestead which cost only $20 in Land-Office fees. Not until the invention of barbed-wire fence brought the cost within

[3] Billington, Ray Allen, *Westward Expansion,* Macmillan, New York, 1960, p. 703.   [4] *Ibid.,* pp. 690–698.

reason could fencing take place on a large scale. Barbed wire was patented in 1874, and the cost was steadily reduced as mass-production techniques increased in efficiency. By 1890, cost of barbed wire was reduced to one-fifth of the original market price in the early 1870's.

Other technological advances such as the windmill for water supply and mechanized farm equipment to cultivate large acreages, facilitated the agricultural conquest of the Great Plains. In the humid east a man and his family could take care of a small farm and produce enough to make a profit. In the dry west where 400 to 600 acres were required, machines had to replace manpower if farming was to succeed. Most of the machines needed were already invented by the time of the Civil War, but costs were high and production was limited because of low demand by the small-scale eastern farms. The growing industries of the east were quick to meet the demand for cheaper and improved plows, planters, and harvesters, and kept pace with the advancing farming frontier on the Great Plains—a process that is still continuing in American agriculture. For example, in the 1890's it was estimated by the United States Commissioner of Labor that the time for producing an acre of wheat was reduced from 61 hours by hand to 3 hours by machine, and the cost from $3.55 to $0.66. Similar reductions were brought about in the time and cost for producing other crops.

Improvement of the processing of agricultural products also was a major factor in making agriculture in the dry west a practical and profitable venture. Wheat produced in the dry lands was of the hard variety, and stone milling devices were not able to cope with it. The old millstones were replaced by rollers, a Hungarian invention, and in 1879 the chilled-iron roller proved successful in enabling large quantities of hard wheat to be processed into flour at milling centers such as Minneapolis, St. Louis, and Kansas City. Also, coupled with the new demands for large quantities of hard wheat flour, mechanized handling of grain at railheads, elevators, and dockside reduced costs, improved farmers' profits, and lowered consumers' costs.

THE GROWTH OF TOWNS AND CITIES

As settlement spread westward, the density of population increased rapidly behind the expanding frontier. Towns and villages were established to serve the growing countryside. These early villages and towns were often founded with the optimistic expectation that they would grow into thriving cities of the future. In the course of development of the North Central States some have fulfilled these early expectations and have become major urban centers, while others have all but disappeared. Still others have remained small towns and villages serving limited areas.

Whether these service centers prospered or failed to grow into major cities depended in large part on fortuitous geographic location with respect to transportation and the capturing of a sizable and prosperous trade area. Many communities prospered because of their location at bulk breaking points where goods had to be transferred from one form of transportation to another, such as from land to water. Others were at important junctions of trade routes, on canals, or at points where major rivers were bridged. Later, locations on railroad main lines stimulated the growth of many cities.

Early Towns in the North Central States. Although the American frontier advanced from east to west, the first real towns in the area which now comprises the North Central States were the early French settlements on the Mississippi River, the Wabash River, and the Great Lakes. Most of these began as forts and fur-trading posts but later grew into towns before the advent of the waves of settlers from the eastern seaboard. Among the earliest of these French towns were Cahokia and Kaskaskia in what is now Illinois. Founded as missions in 1699 at the site of Indian villages, they were transformed in a few years into thriving wilderness towns, attracting farmers and fur traders to their vicinity. Today, Kaskaskia has disappeared, and Cahokia is a small town within the St. Louis metropolitan area. Shortly after the founding of the first Mississippi River towns, Vincennes was established on the Wabash River in what is now southwestern Indiana. Although one of the major centers in frontier days, Vincennes is now a small city of some 18,000 inhabitants.

Of the early French settlements in what is now the area of the North Central States, two have grown into truly great metropolitan centers. In the year 1701, the French established a fort on the present site of the city of Detroit. A hundred years later it was incorporated into a village, and into a city in 1815. Today, it is the center of a metropolitan area of over 3,762,000 people. St. Louis was the other early French settlement destined to become a great city. Founded in 1764 as a fur-trading post, with its advantageous location near the junction of the Mississippi and Missouri rivers it soon became the major settlement of the upper Mississippi. Today, its metropolitan area includes some 2,104,600 people in Missouri and Illinois, and its old historic role as a center of the fur trade is reflected in the fact that it remains to this day the world's leading market center for the raw-fur trade.

Since the fur-trade hinterland of St. Louis lay west of the Mississippi, its position on the west bank gave it an advantage over the east-bank settlements for shipping the furs downriver to New Orleans. Also, the ceding of the Illinois country to England in 1773 caused an exodus of French settlers from the area east of the river to the St. Louis side. By the time the Louisiana Purchase made St. Louis a part of the United States, it was well-established as the major settlement of the region. Later, with the coming of the railroads, St. Louis benefited by being at the entrance of a corridor to the west between the Ozark uplands to the south and the Missouri River to the north. This led St. Louis to develop its major trade connections with the Southwest.

The Ohio River Cities. As American settlement pushed down the Ohio River in the period following the American Revolution, towns were established along the river and along the National Road to the north. Chief among these river towns was Cincinnati, which began in 1789 with the establishment of Fort Washington between the mouths of the Greater Miami and Little Miami rivers. A town soon grew up around the fort, and by 1795 it had developed into a small river village of 500 inhabitants. By 1810, although the fort had been abandoned, Cincinnati had a population of 2,320 and had become a major town in the region.

After 1810, Cincinnati grew rapidly into a true city, with 30,000 inhabitants by 1831, and became the chief port of the Ohio River. In this early period it was the center of what was then the Corn Belt, and its pork-packing industry was the forerunner of what is today the typical corn and hog economy of the modern Corn Belt, the present location of which is to the north and west. Other early industries included cotton spinning, pottery, glassmaking, distilling, and steamboat building. Cincinnati's commerce centered around the shipping of cured, salted, and barreled pork to the South by way of the Ohio and Mississippi rivers to feed the agricultural laborers of the Cotton Belt. It was to maintain its rank as the major pork-packing center of the nation until the Civil War disrupted the southern markets and it was replaced by the developing giant to the north, Chicago. However, it still retains its position as the major city on the Ohio River downstream from Pittsburgh, although the river no longer plays the dominant role in its economy.

Farther downstream another important urban development took place at the Falls of the Ohio, the present site of the Louisville metropolitan area. Although Louisville proper lies outside the North Central States, a considerable part of its metropolitan development lies north of the Ohio River. Louisville was founded in 1779 and by 1820 had grown to a population of nearly 5,000. Five other towns were founded in the first two decades of the nineteenth century in the vicinity of the falls: Shippingport and Portland in Kentucky, and Clarksville, Jeffersonville, and New Albany in Indiana.

The location of Louisville and neighboring communities in Kentucky and Indiana at the Falls of the Ohio was a major factor in their early growth. At low water the falls imposed a virtual break in Ohio River navigation, making it necessary for river boats to stop at Louisville or one of the neighboring towns. Even at high water many boats were unloaded above the falls to lighten their draft and reloaded below. Also, a thriving pilot business was developed to furnish expert guidance through the dangerous chutes. Later, the completion of a canal around the falls made it possible for river traffic to proceed without unloading and loading, but by this time Louisville was an important market center and had become the destination or point of origin for much of the river traffic. Today, Louisville is the center of a metropolitan area of almost three-quarters of a million people, extending north of the Ohio River into Indiana.

The Great Lakes Cities. In addition to the aforementioned city of Detroit, other early lake settlements which grew into major cities are Cleveland and Toledo on Lake Erie, and Chicago and Milwaukee on Lake Michigan.

Cleveland was first settled in 1796 and was incorporated into a village in 1814 with fewer than 100 people. By 1836, it had grown to 6,000 inhabitants and was granted a charter by the Ohio legislature. Its early growth was stimulated by its location at the northern terminus of the Ohio and Erie Canal connecting Lake Erie with the Ohio River. In the 1850's iron ore shipments from the Lake Superior region laid the basis for the development of the iron and steel industry that characterizes the area today. Modern Cleveland is the center of a metropolitan area of over 1,900,000 people, placing it sixteenth in population among metropolitan areas in the United States.

Toledo, originally Port Lawrence, was first settled in 1817 on the site of Fort Industry, which dated from 1795. In 1833 several villages were consolidated into the town of Toledo, and its city charter was granted in 1837. The most important early factor in the growth of the city was the completion of the Miami and Erie Canal and the Wabash and Erie Canal in the 1840's. Since that time the city has been an important port on the Lower Great Lakes. Today, it is a city of over 300,000 population in a metropolitan area of some 460,000, and is a center for automobile parts, glass, petroleum refining, machine tools, steel, and many other diversified industries.

Chicago had a rather unimpressive beginning as Fort Dearborn, established in 1803 and abandoned during the War of 1812. The fort was rebuilt in 1816 and a small village grew up around it to be incorporated into the town of Chicago in 1833. Its original importance stemmed from its location on a passageway from the southern end of Lake Michigan to the Mississippi River via the Chicago River and a portage to the Des Plaines River, a tributary of the Illinois, and thence to the Mississippi. The portage varied from four miles in wet years to more than twenty miles in dry years. In 1820, the population of Chicago was less than 100; but in 1835 the rush to the town began, and by 1848 it had grown to more than 20,000. In 1848, the Illinois-Michigan Canal was opened, and by 1850, the population had increased to above 30,000. The first railroads, which were to make Chicago the world's leading rail center, also arrived in 1848, and by 1860 the city ranked first in size in the State of Illinois with over 112,000 people. By 1871, the year of the great fire, the population exceeded 300,000. The rapid growth of the city during the last century has made it the first city of the North Central States, the second city of the United States, and the eighth city of the world.

North of Chicago, on the west shore of Lake Michigan, is Milwaukee, the eighteenth-ranking metropolitan area of the United States. The area was first settled in 1818, and the town of Milwaukee was established in 1846 by the consolidation of several small towns.

In the 1840's large numbers of German immigrants came to the city, and their cultural influence is still strong. After the completion of rail connections to the west, Milwaukee became a leading market port for grain from the developing farmlands to the west.

Major Cities of the Trans-Mississippi Area. With the exception of St. Louis, the early towns of the North Central States lay to the east of the Mississippi River. One of the major urban centers which developed as a result of the opening of the northern Great Plains and the Upper Mississippi Valley in the later half of the nineteenth century was the twin cities of Minneapolis and St. Paul. St. Paul is the older, having been established at the head of navigation on the Mississippi River about five miles east of its junction with the Minnesota River. In 1849, St. Paul became the capital of Minnesota, and in the census of 1850 it had 1,112 inhabitants.

A few miles to the northwest of St. Paul were the Falls of St. Anthony, just below Nicolet Island in the Mississippi River. Here, water power was available, and the island afforded the easiest crossing of the river. The town of St. Anthony was established on the east bank at this point and became an important sawmilling center with the development of lumbering to the north. From St. Anthony, lumber products were taken the short distance to St. Paul, which became a great lumber exporting center and supplier for the logging industry.

In the 1850's, Minneapolis was founded on the west bank of the Mississippi and by 1880 had annexed St. Anthony and was larger than St. Paul. While St. Paul was oriented to the lumber area to the north and the dairy region to the east, Minneapolis developed a hinterland to the west, which included the rapidly developing grain areas of the northern plains. It was destined to become one of the great milling centers of the continent.

Farther south and west is the metropolitan center of Kansas City, where the Missouri River bends northward. The earliest settlement in this area was Independence, Missouri, established in 1831. In the

early years it was the main starting point on the Oregon and Santa
Fe trails. However, with the opening of Kansas to settlement in
the early 1850's, Independence was eclipsed by the newer town of
Kansas City, which became the major city in the area and reached
a population of 32,000 by 1870. Railroads to the southwest also were
important to the development of the Kansas City area with its
favored location at the western end of the corridor between the
Ozarks and the Missouri River, a situation similar to that of St.
Louis at the eastern end of the same corridor. By 1960, the Kansas
City metropolitan area had a population of 1,092,545, the largest
urban concentration in the North Central States west of St. Louis.

The Great Plains, with a sparse population compared to that of
the humid east, has fewer and more widely spaced urban areas,
most of these the outgrowth of the westward expansion of the railroads during the later half of the nineteenth century. It is not until
the western margin of the plains is reached that an urban center
of considerable magnitude is again encountered. This is the Denver
metropolitan area at the foot of the Front Range of the Rocky
Mountains.

Denver was founded in 1858 as a result of the influx of gold
seekers during the Pike's Peak gold rush of that year. Mining continued as the principal economic activity until its rapid decline
after 1890. Agriculture, based on irrigation, developed in the
Colorado Piedmont to supply the mining camps and was given
added impetus by the arrival of the first railroad to Denver in
1870. Today, Denver is the leading city of the High Plains, as well
as the economic focus of the southern Rocky Mountains. It is a
highly diversified manufacturing center and the headquarters for
more than 200 government agencies and several military establishments. The city with its adjacent metropolitan area has a population of about 930,000.

Locational Factors in Retrospect. The sampling of cities presented
above is sufficient to give some basis for generalization about the

locational factors involved in their early growth and subsequent development into important urban centers in the North Central States. In the humid east it is not coincidental that most of the centers are located on rivers, most of which were navigable at least at the time of settlement, or on other water routes such as lakes or canals. Most are at bulk breaking points where goods were transferred from land to water or water to land. In all cases, the water routes were eventually supplemented or replaced by railroads.

Original site locations were often determined by forts, but the rapid westward movement of the frontier made the importance of these military centers short-lived and of little significance in the ultimate development of the cities. A few major centers owe their development almost entirely to the railroads, an example being Indianapolis, which was not on a navigable waterway. In the Great Plains area, the growth of most settlements depended on rails, thus supporting the thesis that railroads were the real conquerors of the plains. A few like Denver owe their early start to mining, and some remain as mining centers, particularly in the Great Lakes iron mining region and in the important coal producing areas.

POPULATION DISTRIBUTION TODAY

The North Central States includes about 30 percent of the total land area of the conterminous United States. This area also contains about 30 percent of the total population of the United States. The overall population density in the North Central States is about 59 persons per square mile, while that of the 48 states is about 60 per square mile. A further indication that the area is representative of the country is the fact that the ratio of urban to rural population is almost exactly the same as for the whole United States: 70 percent urban to 30 percent rural. However, these overall figures mask the great diversity in population density within the North Central States.

In general, population density decreases from east to west. Ohio had an overall population density of about 237 people per square mile according to the Census of 1960, the highest of any of the North Central States, while Wyoming had the lowest with only about 3.4 persons per square mile. All states lying east of the Mississippi River, with the exception of Minnesota and Wisconsin, have population densities well over 100 persons per square mile, while those to the west of the river are considerably below 100. The population characteristics of the states comprising the area are summarized in Table 2.

The high population densities in the east are, in part, explained by the presence of large metropolitan areas and more intensive farming. However, rural densities show less contrast, with Ohio again leading with 63 per square mile, while Wyoming has only 1.5 per square mile. It should be pointed out that the figures for urban-vs.-rural population as indicated in the United States Census can be misleading because much of the rural population, particularly in the densely settled eastern states, is rural nonfarm, generally in rural hamlets and villages with fewer than 2,500 people. The intensity of agricultural settlement is better illustrated by the population actually engaged in farming in relation to the land in farms. These figures show much less contrast from east to west, with Ohio having eight persons engaged in agriculture per square mile of farmland in 1962; Illinois, 4.6; Iowa and Minnesota, each 5.5; the Dakotas, about 1.3; Kansas and Nebraska, about 2; Colorado, 1.1; and Montana and Wyoming, less than one (Table 2).

This distribution of population reflects, in large part, the physical environment, particularly climate. In the humid east the agricultural settlement early reached a considerable density, and numerous towns grew up as service centers to serve the countryside. Later, many of the settlements grew into manufacturing centers with the westward spread of the manufacturing belt. Farther west, where low rainfall made farming more extensive, towns were farther apart.

Recent Trends in Population Distribution. As in the remainder of the United States, urban population has been growing rapidly at the expense of the rural population. By 1960, the urban population

TABLE 2

Population Characteristics, North Central States, 1960 Census of Population

STATE	Total Population 1960	Population Density Per Sq. Mi.	Rural Density Per Sq. Mi.	Density of Pop. Engaged in Agriculture Per Sq. Mi. Farmland	Percent Urban	Percent Growth 1900–1960	Percent Growth 1950–1960
Ohio	9,706,397	237	63	8.0	73.4	133.4	22.1
Michigan	7,823,194	137	37	7.4	73.4	223.1	22.8
Indiana	4,662,498	129	49	7.0	62.4	85.3	18.5
Illinois	10,081,158	180	35	4.6	80.7	109.1	15.7
Wisconsin	3,951,777	72	26	8.0	63.8	91.0	15.1
Minnesota	3,413,864	43	16	5.5	62.2	95.0	14.5
Iowa	2,757,537	49	23	5.5	53.0	23.6	5.2
Missouri	4,319,813	63	23	5.1	66.6	39.0	9.2
Kansas	2,178,611	27	10	1.9	61.0	48.2	14.3
South Dakota	680,514	8.9	5.4	1.2	39.3	69.4	4.3
North Dakota	632,446	9.1	5.9	1.3	35.2	98.1	2.1
Nebraska	1,411,330	18	12	2.0	54.3	32.2	6.5
Montana	674,767	4.6	2.3	0.3	50.2	177.8	14.2
Wyoming	330,066	3.4	1.5	0.3	56.8	254.8	13.6
Colorado	1,753,947	17	4.5	1.1	73.3	224.8	32.4
Total N. Cent. States	54,377,919	59	15.6	—	70.0	98.0	8.0
Total, U.S.A. (48 States)	179,323,175	60	13.2	—	69.9	135.5	18.5

had risen to over 80 percent in Illinois, reflecting the great Chicago metropolitan area, while only two states, North and South Dakota, had fewer urban residents than rural. Even Iowa, often considered the "typical" agricultural state, has over half of its population classed as urban by the Census, and only 11 percent actually are engaged directly in farming. Of the 15 states, only North and South Dakota, with 14 and 13 percent, respectively, employed in agriculture, exceeded the Iowa percentage. Nebraska is the same as Iowa, and in all other states the percentage is less than 10 percent, with the lowest percentage of 2.3 found in Ohio. This trend reflects the growing efficiency of agriculture and the increasing attractiveness of urban life, particularly to the less successful members of the farming population.

Of special significance in the distribution of population is the size and location of the centers of urban concentration, termed *Standard Metropolitan Statistical Areas (SMSA)* by the United States Bureau of the Census. An SMSA is defined by the Census as a county containing at least one central city with a population of 50,000 or more inhabitants, or twin cities which are contiguous and have a combined population of at least 50,000. Two or more adjacent counties, each with a central city meeting the above criteria, and with the cities within 20 miles of each other, are included in the same SMSA unless there is evidence that they are not economically integrated. A number of other criteria are used to determine whether other contiguous counties will be included in the SMSA; for example, an adjacent county is included if at least 75 percent of the labor force is nonagricultural.

The SMSA is a more realistic unit than the political city, since urban political boundaries often bear little relationship to total urbanization. Although all of the SMSA's within the North Central States showed increases between the 1950 and 1960 Census years, many of the central cities have shown a decline in population, an indication of the flight to the suburbs. It is interesting to note that the greatest loss from the central city has occurred in the larger

SMSA's, while most of the smaller ones have shown increases in the number of inhabitants in the central city. However, this growth has often been at a lesser rate than in the area as a whole. In the eight SMSA's with more than a million people, only two central cities, Kansas City and Milwaukee, had an increase in population between 1950 and 1960. These are also the smallest of the million-class SMSA's within the North Central States. The greatest percentage loss (14 percent) within the central city occurred in St. Louis (Table 3). St. Louis is a classic example of a city hemmed in and in the process of being strangled by its suburbs.

The flight from the central city to the suburbs has imposed financial problems on the urban governments of these cities which are called upon to provide increasing public services for a growing population with a declining tax base. This problem is further intensified because the more affluent within the population are the first to move to the suburbs. Some city governments have imposed a tax on the income earned within the city to force the suburban dwellers to pay a share of the costs of maintaining the services in the central city where they work but do not live.

Today, the SMSA's within the North Central States contain over 63 percent of the total population, with those exceeding a million inhabitants in size accounting for some 35 percent, and those smaller about 28 percent. The increasing importance of these major metropolitan areas as places of residence is further emphasized by the increase in their percentage of the total population, from 52 percent in 1950 to 63 percent in 1960. The percentage increase in the million-class group is also spectacular, with 35 percent of the total in 1960, compared to only 27 percent in 1950.

Of the 225 SMSA's in the United States, 67 (30 percent) are located in the North Central States. The area also contains eight of the 24 SMSA's with more than one million inhabitants. As would be expected, the location of these metropolitan areas reflects the general population distribution discussed earlier in this chapter. Most of the SMSA's are east of the Mississippi River, and only one

TABLE 3

Changes in Population in Standard Metropolitan Statistical Areas of over a Million Population and their Central Cities, North Central States, 1950–1960

City	Population of SMSA		% Change	Population of Central City		% Change Central City
	1950	1960	SMSA 1950–60	1950	1960	1950–1960
Chicago	5,177,868	6,220,913	+12.0	3,620,962	3,550,404	−2.0
Detroit	3,016,197	3,762,360	+12.5	1,849,568	1,670,144	−10.0
St. Louis	1,755,334	2,104,669	+12.0	856,796	750,026	−14.0
Cleveland	1,523,574	1,909,483	+12.5	914,808	876,050	−4.0
Minneapolis-St. Paul	1,151,053	1,482,030	+13.0	833,067	796,283	−5.0
Cincinnati	1,023,245	1,268,479	+12.5	503,998	502,550	−0.5
Milwaukee	980,309	1,232,731	+12.5	637,392	741,324	+17.0
Kansas City	848,655	1,092,545	+13.0	456,622	475,539	+4.0

in the million class, Kansas City, is entirely west of the river. Two, Minneapolis-St. Paul and St. Louis, lie on both sides of the Mississippi. The central part of the Great Plains contains no cities of sufficient size to be included in the SMSA's, but there are a number along the eastern margin of the plains (Fargo-Moorhead, Sioux Falls, Sioux City, Omaha, Lincoln, St. Joseph, Topeka, Kansas City, and Wichita), and along the western margin in the Rocky Mountain piedmont (Pueblo, Colorado Springs, Denver, Billings, and Great Falls).

Interregional Movements of Population. Much emphasis has been placed in recent years on the migration of rural Southerners, particularly Negroes, to other regions of the United States. The large cities of the North Central States have received increasing numbers of rural migrants over the last several decades. John Fraser Hart, in his study of the changing distribution of the American Negro, concludes that there have been three major streams of Negro migration in the United States: (1) from the South Atlantic States to the Northeast; (2) from the Delta, the Black Belt of Alabama, and the entire State of Mississippi to the east North Central States, particularly to the urban centers such as St. Louis, Chicago, Cleveland and Detroit; and (3) from southern Arkansas, northern Louisiana, and eastern Texas to the west-coast metropolitan centers of Los Angeles, San Francisco, and Seattle.[5] Of course there has been considerable cross-migration among these streams.

This northward movement of the Negro has been particularly impressive since the increase in urban concentration of Negroes is more obvious because of race than is the movement of the white population. Thus, the findings of the United States Department of Agriculture in a special study of the characteristics of the United States population by farm and nonfarm origins are particularly interesting. Contrary to the general impression of interregional migra-

[5] Hart, John Fraser, "The Changing Distribution of the American Negro," *Annals of the Association of American Geographers,* Vol. 50, No. 3, Sept. 1960, pp. 242–266.

tion of farm-born population, the highest rate has been from the North Central States and not the South. From this region 17.8 percent of the farm-born in 1958 had moved to other regions, compared with 21.7 percent of the nonfarm-born. The Western States have been the destination of 80 percent of the farm-born Midwesterners who have migrated to other regions, as they have for the nonfarm migrants. At the time of the Department of Agriculture's study, only 15.7 percent of the farm-born adults of the South had moved to other regions, compared with 23.9 percent of the nonfarm-born Southerners.[6]

Political Implications of the Population Shift. Aside from the demographic and economic effects of the rural to urban migration in the North Central States and the remainder of the country, the political implications are beginning to be felt. The area has long been the stronghold of rural-dominated state legislatures and Congressional Representatives with a strong rural bias. Much of this rural bias has stemmed from the failure to redistrict the states along lines taking into account the shifts from rural to urban majorities. Until the recent decisions of the U.S. Supreme Court calling for "one man, one vote," the rural resident's vote counted much more heavily than that of his city neighbor. The rural dominance of state and national government has meant a very favorable climate for agriculture in the United States and a tendency to ignore urban problems. The long delay before a Department of Urban Affairs was finally established and the vast resources and budgets of the Department of Agriculture are evidence of the rural bias of Congress. With changes in the voting power of urban-vs.-rural interests, we may be on the brink of a completely different approach to rural and urban problems.

[6] U.S. Department of Agriculture, Economic and Statistical Analysis Division, *Characteristics of the U.S. Population by Farm and Nonfarm Origin,* Agricultural Economic Report No. 66, Washington, D.C., 1964.

The Midwesterner. Today, the people of the North Central States represent a successful blending of the many groups that have settled in the area during the last century-and-a-half. The Old American stock that formed the first waves of settlement from the eastern seaboard was joined by the great influx of immigrants from Europe during the closing decades of the nineteenth century and the early decades of the twentieth century. The influence of all of these groups has blended to produce the characteristic personality of the Midwest. Few areas of comparable size have such little variation in the spoken idiom. The resident of Ohio speaks with accents which would not mark him as an outsider in most other parts of the North Central States except along the southern transition. Today, Midwestern English represents the "standard" English of the United States.

The immigrants have left their mark on certain communities and areas. Detroit and other large cities have their Polish, Italian, and other ethnic neighborhoods. German influence is still strong in Milwaukee and St. Louis. Minnesota retains many cultural traditions of the Scandinavian settlers and the Finnish *sauna* is a part of the cultural landscape in the Upper Great Lakes area.

Despite their diverse ancestral backgrounds, the presentday descendants of the immigrants and the Old Americans share a common culture. Most of the second and third generations have lost the native tongue of their parents and grandparents because the desire to Americanize has been strong. The writer saw evidence of this a few years ago when he attended an evening class in the Danish language in Des Moines. Although most of the class participants were from Danish family backgrounds, almost none of them knew more than a few words and phrases of Danish.

Unfortunately, the most recent immigrant, the southern Negro, has not fared so well in being assimilated into the mainstream of Midwestern culture. Marked by his race and met by prejudice, often from the descendants of immigrant groups who were themselves subjected to the same discrimination a generation or so ago, he has been forced to live in ghettos and has found it difficult to advance his economic and social status. Unquestionably, the problem of race relations is the most serious one facing an area that has prided itself as a "melting pot" of diverse peoples.

3   *Resources of the Land: Agriculture*

ALTHOUGH most of the states comprising the North Central States area are no longer predominantly agricultural, the area still holds first place in agricultural production among the nation's farming regions. Unquestionably, the area contains some of the most productive agricultural land on earth. In spite of the decline in the number of people engaged in farming, the level of production has risen continuously as technology and capital investment have replaced manpower in producing food and industrial crops for the United States market and for export.

In 1964, the area produced more than two-fifths of the total farm production of the 48 conterminous states, based on the cash receipts from marketing and government payments. The Corn Belt States alone produced almost one-fourth of the total, the part of the Great Plains that lies within the North Central States 11 percent, and the Lake States 9 percent, for a total of over 43 percent of the national production. Table 4 summarizes the cash receipts from agriculture by regions as designated by the Department of Agriculture. The footnotes to Table 4 give a listing of the states included in each agriculture region by the Department of Agriculture.

THE AGRICULTURAL REVOLUTION

The technological revolution that has transformed American agriculture within the last two decades has been more dramatic

59

than changes in any other segment of the economy. The role of technology in the settlement of the Great Plains and prairies was emphasized in the chapter on settlement. This was the beginning

TABLE 4

Cash Receipts from Farm Marketing and Government Payments, by Regions (48 States), 1964

Region	Cash Receipts (Million Dollars)	Percent of 48 States	
Northeast [1]	3,151	8.1	
Lake States [2]	*3,646*	*9.1*	North Central
Corn Belt [3]	*8,893*	*23.0*	States
Northern Plains [4]	*4,331*	*11.1*	(43.2%)
Appalachians [5]	3,288	8.5	
Southeast [6]	2,947	7.5	
Delta States [7]	2,176	5.6	
Southern Plains [8]	3,170	8.1	
Mountain States [9]	2,726	7.0	
Pacific States [10]	4,740	12.0	
Total (48 States)	39,068	100.0	

[1] Maine, New Hampshire, Vermont, Mass., R.I., Conn., N.Y., N.J., Penn., Del., Maryland
[2] Mich., Wis., Minn.
[3] Ohio, Ind., Ill., Missouri, Iowa
[4] N.D., S.D., Neb., Kan.
[5] Va., W.Va., N.C., Ken., Tenn.
[6] S.C., Ga., Fla., Ala.
[7] Miss., Ark., La.
[8] Okla., Tex.
[9] Mont., Idaho, Wyo., Col., N.M., Ariz., Utah, Nev.
[10] Wash., Oregon, Calif.

Source: U.S. Department of Agriculture, *The Balance Sheet for Agriculture,* Agricultural Information Bull. No. 290, Washington, D.C., Sept. 1965.

of the technological revolution. Today, this revolution is still in progress and surpluses of agricultural commodities are a continuing problem for the first time in the history of civilization. Some authorities consider this condition of agricultural surplus as a temporary situation that will be wiped out by population increase. Nowhere is this great technological breakthrough more in evidence than in the more productive parts of the North Central States.

Beginning in the mid-nineteenth century with the use of machines powered by horses and mules, the mechanization of agriculture had progressed by World War II to the stage where the use of inanimate power was well on the way to replacing animal power. The decline of animal power is dramatically illustrated by the reduction of the number of horses and mules on farms from the peak number of 26.7 million in 1917 to only 3.1 million in 1960. Since 1960, the Department of Agriculture has discontinued estimating the number of draft animals because it is insignificant. With the reduction of the number of work animals on farms there also has been a reduction in the number of acres used for producing feed for these animals. In 1910, some 72 million acres of farmland were necessary to feed the horses and mules on American farms. As recently as 1940, about 42 million acres were so used, but by 1961 only 4 million acres were needed to feed the remaining draft animals.

During the period when animal power was declining in importance in American agriculture, manpower also was being replaced by machines powered by internal combustion engines and electricity. The major replacement for the horse was the tractor, the all-purpose source of power on most farms. In 1910, it is estimated that there were only one thousand tractors on farms in the United States. By 1932, the number had exceeded one million, and by 1961 it had reached 4.7 million. Today's farmer must be, among other things, a master mechanic and electrician, and has more industrial skills than most urban industrial workers. Because of the reduction in the number of farms and the increase in farm size, machines are becoming larger, and a decline in the numbers of some types of farm machines has been noted. For example, the number of grain combines reached a peak in 1959, while the number of farms with milking-machines has declined since 1954. However, pickup bailers, field forage harvesters, cornpickers, and motor trucks all have increased in number since 1954.

This great emphasis on mechanization has had parallels in other forms of technology that have been brought about by the application of science to agriculture. Major factors in the accelerated rate of productivity increase which has occurred since the late 1930's have been the introduction of hybrid corn, about which more will be said later, and the rapid increase in the use of chemical fertilizers. The principal plant nutrients added to the soil in the form of commercial fertilizers are nitrogen, phosphoric oxide (P_2O_5), and potash (K_2O). In 1910, the total of these plant nutrients used in American agriculture amounted to only 856,000 tons.[1] By 1963, the amount was 10.5 million tons, more than a 12-fold increase. In the North Central States the increase in fertilizer use has been even more spectacular. In 1910, this area used only 185,000 tons of nutrients compared with 4.8 million tons in 1963, twenty-six times as much, or more than twice the amount of increase nationally. For many years the Southeast led in the use of fertilizers; but since 1951 the Corn Belt States of Ohio, Indiana, Illinois, Iowa, and Missouri have been in the forefront of fertilizer use. By 1963, the Corn Belt States accounted for almost 30 percent of the national consumption (Table 5).

The phenomenal increase in the productivity of agriculture is even more impressive against the background of declining agricultural population, farm numbers, and acres of cropland. In 1910, some 317 million acres of cropland were harvested in the United States. The acreage increased gradually until the peak year 1932, when 361 million acres of crops were harvested. By 1961, this acreage had dropped below the 1910 level, when the harvested acreage was only 297 million acres. However, in 1961 the produc-

[1] These figures represent the total available plant-nutrient content of commercial fertilizers used. Total tonnage of fertilizers is considerably greater since it includes inert materials.

tivity per acre was 1.7 times what it was in 1910, and in the North Central States the major increases in yields have come since 1939.

TABLE 5

Fertilizer Use by Nutrient Content, North Central States, 1963,
in million tons

Region and State	Nitrogen N	Phosphoric Oxide P_2O_5	Potash K_2O	Total	Percent of Total U.S. Consumption
Corn Belt					
Ohio	.145	.182	.162	.489	
Indiana	.233	.211	.249	.693	
Illinois	.362	.276	.267	.905	
Iowa	.275	.204	.120	.599	
Missouri	.184	.116	.108	.408	
Subtotal	1.199	.989	.906	3.094	29.5
Lake States					
Michigan	.095	.129	.119	.343	
Wisconsin	.041	.083	.122	.246	
Minnesota	.095	.168	.101	.364	
Subtotal	.231	.380	.342	.953	9.0
Northern Plains					
North Dakota	.025	.066	.002	.093	
South Dakota	.022	.018	.002	.042	
Nebraska	.226	.057	.006	.289	
Kansas	.165	.100	.011	.276	
Subtotal	.438	.241	.021	.700	6.7
Total for North Cent. States				4.747	45.2

Source: Agricultural Statistics, 1965, U.S. Government Printing Office, Superintendent of Documents, Washington, D.C., 1966.

In the Corn Belt States the increase in per-acre yield between 1939 and 1961 was on the order of 52 percent, while in the Lake States it was 46 percent. Although the yield in the Northern Great Plains States in 1961 was 100 percent greater than that of 1939, it is much more difficult to arrive at a meaningful measure of increase based on the comparison of individual years of production because of the much greater role played by weather, which results in large fluctuations in yields from year to year. If the weather factor is eliminated statistically, the increase in wheat yields between 1939 and 1961 was about 49 percent.

Not only has yield per acre increased over the last half century, but yield per man-hour has increased even more rapidly. It required 36 years, from 1910 to 1946, for the productivity per man-hour to double; yet eight years later in 1954 it had doubled again, and a mere seven years later in 1961, it had more than doubled again. Thus, we have an increase at an accelerated rate. In the Corn Belt States between 1939 and 1961 the total man-hours of labor used for farm work per year declined from 3.4 million to 1.6 million, only 47 percent as much.

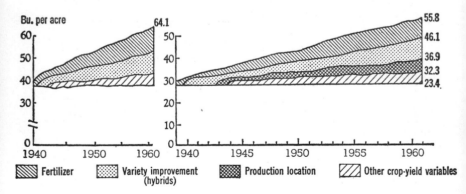

*Corn yield increases due to various factors of crop technology.**

* From L. W. Auer et al., "Influence of Crop Technology on Yield," *Iowa Farm Science,* March, 1966.

The expenditure of labor and use of land, power and machinery, fertilizers, feed, seed, livestock, etc., are referred to by economists as "inputs." When these are measured against the "outputs" of agriculture, the ratio is a measure of productivity. We have seen that the major proportion of total inputs has tended to shift from labor and land to fertilizers, mechanization, and improved seeds, which call for greater capital expenditures. While inputs have increased, the output per unit of input has increased more rapidly. In 1870, the output per unit of input (productivity) was only about 46 percent of what it was in 1961.

The significance of the output from the farm sector of the American economy is summarized by the U.S. Department of Agriculture in commenting on the persons supplied by one farm worker:

> During 1961, each farmworker in the U.S. produced enough food, fiber, and tobacco to supply himself and more than 26 other persons. This was almost 7 times the number of consumers supplied with agricultural products by one farmworker in 1820. *Almost half of this increase came in the last decade of the 140-year period* . . . .[2]

PROBLEMS OF AGRICULTURE

The statistics indicating the remarkable technological development of American agriculture should not mislead the reader into thinking that this means prosperity throughout the farm sector of the nation's economy. During the period when these rapid technological advances were taking place, the total net income from farming declined, and the per capita income increased much more slowly than that for the nonfarm sector of our population. Between 1947–1949 and 1959 the total disposable income of the nonfarm population increased by 83 percent, while the per capita income increased by 40 percent because of the increase in population. Meanwhile, the

[2] U.S. Department of Agriculture, *Changes in Farm Production Efficiency, A Summary Report, 1962,* Statistical Bull. No. 233, September, 1962. Italics supplied.

total net income in the farm sector declined by 20 percent, while, because of a decrease in farm population, the individual income increased some 16 percent. Thus, we see that farm incomes have not kept pace with the general growth rate of the economy.

At the same time the farmer is caught in a price squeeze, because to farm by modern standards requires a large capital investment in machinery, fertilizers, etc.—the prices of which are rising faster than the farmer's income. Therefore, the average farmer is receiving a smaller return on his investment than is the case in most other industries. This situation can be interpreted as an over-commitment of our national resources to agriculture, thereby reducing prices and resulting in over-production. Since the domestic demand for farm products does not increase in proportion to income or in response to lower prices, other outlets such as exports must be found, or more of our resources must be diverted from agriculture.

Efforts of the government to solve the farm problem by price support and acreage allotments have not proven too successful until recently. When a modern farmer has been faced with the prospect of fewer acres to farm, his response has been to concentrate his capital resources on the smaller acreage; and, in many cases, he actually has succeeded in producing more on less land. The marginal farmer who is forced out of agriculture by the economic pressures also has little effect on the total production except to raise it. His land usually is taken over by a more successful, and thus more efficient, operator, who generally turns the substandard farmlands into productive units at a higher efficiency level, thereby adding additional bushels to the total. Logically, production limits rather than acreage limits would solve the problem more efficiently, but this has not proved to be politically acceptable.

With a major part of the world's peoples subsisting on substandard diets, it would seem logical to divert surplus American production to those areas where food is in short supply. This has been done successfully on a limited basis, as illustrated by wheat shipments to India and other parts of the world.

The farm programs between 1961 and 1966 proved more successful in limiting production. By the end of the 1966 harvest season, wheat reserves had fallen to a low level compared to the one-billion-bushel surpluses of former years. Faced with what was considered to be a dangerously low reserve of wheat, the Department of Agriculture set about to encourage increased acreage and higher wheat production for 1967. The 1967 program also called for an increase in the production of feed grains in response to low reserves.

The farm sector of the economy responded to the efforts to increase productivity and the 1967 wheat crop was over twenty percent above the previous year. However, fear expressed by some farmers that increased production would mean lower prices seems to have been justified. Farm prices were generally lower in late 1967 than in the preceding year when farm income reached record highs. Increasing discontent is evident in certain sectors of the agricultural community over the tightening of the cost-price squeeze and lagging farm income in relation to urban earnings. Although 1966 was a record year for farm income, the per-capita disposable income from all sources for the farm population was still only 66 percent of the average for the nonfarm population. Declining prices for farm products and increased cost of farm operations during 1967 contributed to the growing rural discontent.

What the future holds for agriculture in the North Central States is problematical. In this area, particularly in the Corn Belt, the family farm has been able to adjust to the changing economic conditions. However, this has necessitated an increase in operation unit size, and many less efficient family farms have been absorbed by their more efficient neighbors. Today, the family farm bears only a vague resemblance to the nostalgic image of the family farm of old. In reality, the modern family farm is more analogous to a small business than to the stereotype. Increased efficiency through mechanization has permitted the single operator to increase the size of his operations with a minimum of outside help. Whether the family farm can survive into the future and adjust to the steadily increasing demands for capital investment remains to be seen.

Already signs of the growth of corporate or industrial farms are making their appearance. There is fear among Corn Belt farmers that their traditional role as feeders of livestock for market may be threatened by the rapid growth of giant feeder lots which fatten range cattle and send them directly to market, thus bypassing the corn farmer and his traditional function as a middleman between the western range and the packing plants. Considerable capital for the development of these large feeding operations seems to be coming from the meat-packing companies, and farm-sponsored legislation to curtail the involvement of corporations in livestock feeding may be submitted to Congress. Should these large-scale corporate operations continue to develop, some observers believe that it could spell the end of family farming as we have known it in the past.

THE ROLE OF EDUCATION IN AGRICULTURE

American agriculture was fortunate to develop in a period of world history when scientific experimentation was making possible a break with old patterns of technology, many of which had existed since antiquity. This new philosophy of science was applied to American agriculture even in the Colonial period, when many gentlemen farmers joined agricultural societies and experimented in horticulture and farming practices. However, to bear fruit the results of these experiments must be made available to the common farmer, who traditionally has been conservative. The answer to this problem was obviously education. The faith of the early settlers in public education has produced a literate farm population in most parts of the North Central States, and has simplified the dissemination of technical information.

The early farm organizations and the popular farm journals were a step in the direction of national agricultural organizations, state departments of agriculture, a federal department of agriculture, and a nationwide system of state agricultural colleges and experiment stations. Paul H. Johnstone, writing in the 1940 Yearbook of Agriculture, points out that:

The existence of a growing body of institutions deliberately and directly devoted to the alteration and improvement of agriculture is therefore a fact of tremendous significance in American history. It has meant that there has been within the agricultural world itself a force constantly working to overcome traditional inertias and to direct agriculture into new paths.[3]

The first major step in furthering scientific experimentation and education in agriculture was the Land Grant Act (Morrill Act) of 1862, which resulted in the establishment of the land-grant colleges. Many of the outstanding state universities of the North Central States had their beginnings as land-grant institutions, and continue to serve the cause of scientific agriculture as well as the needs of the nonfarm population. The work of these institutions was furthered by the establishment of federal-state cooperative experiment stations in 1887. Today, the research of these experiment stations is made available to the farmers by the Agricultural Extension Service, which was established in 1914 as a federal-state cooperative venture.

Today's progressive farmers and ranchers depend on the experiment stations for new techniques, crop varieties, and advice on the economics of farm operation. In addition, the farmer himself often is trained in agriculture through the Smith-Hughes Vocational Education courses in high school, or perhaps he is a graduate of one of the great land-grant colleges or universities. Many of the highly successful farmers may even have advanced degrees in agriculture or agricultural economics. An acquaintance of the writer operates an 800-acre, model livestock farm in the Corn Belt, has a master's degree in economics, and was at one time an instructor in a large state university. Unquestionably, education would have to be listed at the top of any list of factors contributing to the present high level of agriculture in the North Central States.

[3] U.S. Department of Agriculture, "An Historical Survey of American Agriculture," *Farmers in a Changing World,* 1940 Yearbook of Agriculture, Washington, D.C., 1940.

FARM LIFE TODAY

The gap between the way of life on the farms of the North Central States and that in the cities has narrowed. There is little difference in the general standard of living of the typical farm family and that of the middle-class urbanite. The modern farmhouse is comparable to the city home except that the farmhouse is probably larger. Today, 98 percent of all U.S. farms have electricity, and 75 percent have complete indoor plumbing. These percentages in the Corn Belt and the better farming areas of the North Central States are higher than the national averages, reflecting the better economic conditions.

The farmer watches the same TV programs as his city neighbor, and farm radio programs form an important link in communications between the farmer and the experiment stations. The radio keeps the farmer informed about farm market conditions with daily market reports. Mass communications have played an important role in eliminating the cultural differences between urban and rural life.

Like the urban resident, the farmer is dependent on others for most of the necessities of life. Food is no longer produced in large quantities for use by the farm family. The farmer depends on the supermarket for such traditionally home-produced products as milk, dairy products, eggs, meat, and bread. It is the rare farm that keeps chickens or dairy cows for home supply, unless it is a specialized dairy or poultry farm.

Culturally, the farmer is becoming more like the urban resident. He attends motion pictures, theaters, and sporting events in nearby cities. He may travel many miles by automobile or chartered bus to attend special functions such as basketball tournaments. The successful farmer vacations in the same areas as his city counterpart and participates in the same recreational activities. On the streets of the towns and cities, or at the vacation resorts, the farmer dresses, acts, and speaks like the urbanite from whom he is indistinguishable.

The automobile has been a major factor in the breakdown of the past isolation of farm life. When the states were formed, county size was often determined by the travel time to the county seat plus return on the same day, by horse-drawn conveyance. Today, the farmer may visit the county seat and return in a matter of a few hours over distances that once required a full-day's travel.

Surveys of marketing and commuting habits have shown that the Iowa resident regularly travels as much as 50 miles, one way, to shop or work. In fact, it has been found that the areas making major contributions to the economy of cities of 10,000 or more population in the state fall within the 50-mile driving distance from the centers of the central cities.[4] On the other hand, the Iowa farmer or small-town resident thinks little of driving halfway across the state to shop in Des Moines or Omaha, or to attend special events. Occasionally, he may even drive or fly to Chicago. With the completion of the high-speed Interstate Highway System, such trips undoubtedly will increase in frequency.

Increased mobility of the rural population has had far-reaching effects on the service centers of the North Central States. The small hamlets and villages, with their limited retail and service establishments, have experienced a decline in economic activity and population. The larger towns and cities of the region have prospered and grown with the expansion of their trade areas at the expense of the smaller centers.

[4] Fox, Karl A., and Kumar, T. Krishna, "Delineating Functional Economic Areas for Development Programs," in Iowa State Univ. Center for Agricultural and Economic Development, *Research and Education for Regional and Area Development,* Iowa State Univ. Press, Ames, 1966, pp. 13–55.

4 *Agricultural Regions of the North Central States*

I n an area the size of the North Central States, with its regional contrasts in topography, climate, and soils it is inevitable that considerable regional specialization in agriculture will occur. On the basis of land use the Department of Agriculture recognizes sixteen regions within the conterminous United States, eight of which lie wholly or partly within the North Central States. These eight are: (1) the Midland Feed Region, including the widely recognized Corn Belt; (2) the Northern Great Plains, which extend northward into Canada; (3) the Winter Wheat and Grazing Area of the Southern Great Plains, extending southward into Oklahoma and Texas; (4) the Grazing and Irrigated Region, a small part of which lies in the Colorado Piedmont, although most lies to the west of the area about which we are concerned; (5) the East-Central Uplands, stretching from the Ozarks in the west through the Ohio Valley to the Appalachian Plateaus in the east; (6) the Mississippi Delta Region,[1] the northernmost part of which includes the Missouri "Bootheel" and a small part of Illinois; (7) the Northeast, a part of which is located in northeastern Ohio south of Lake Erie; and (8) the Northern Great Lakes Region, in the northern

---

[1] The term "Delta" is used to refer to the broad alluvial valley of the Mississippi River between the southern extremity of the State of Illinois and the Gulf of Mexico, and is therefore more extensive than the Mississippi Delta in the topographic sense.

parts of Minnesota, Wisconsin, and Michigan. These regions and their subregions are shown on Figure 5.

Each of these regions has a combination of climate, soils, and terrain which gives rise to contrasting agricultural systems with different crops and problems of land use. Although these regions form a convenient framework for discussing agriculture, it should be borne in mind that conditions within a single region are not uniform and that soils and climate vary considerably within each region. Also, in passing from one region to another, a zone of transition is often encountered, although the borders appear as sharp lines on the map. Some of the boundaries are determined primarily by climate, especially the boundary between the humid east and the dry west, or the Humid Subtropical south and the Humid Continental north. Other boundaries are the result of rather abrupt changes in topography or soils, such as those between the young glacial plains and the older glacial drift areas, or the East Central Uplands and the alluvial land of the Mississippi Delta Region. The boundaries are, therefore, smoothed lines on the map that should not be endowed with more accuracy than they actually represent.

THE MIDLAND FEED REGION

The Midland Feed Region includes all of the state of Iowa and parts of North Dakota, South Dakota, Minnesota, Wisconsin, Michigan, Ohio, Indiana, Illinois, Missouri, Nebraska, and Kansas. Incorporating the well-known Corn Belt, as well as fringing transitional areas, this region is the true heartland of American agriculture. With 220 million acres and 11.5 percent of the total land area of the United States, excluding Alaska and Hawaii, the region contains more than 34 percent of the total cropland. It produces over two-thirds of the corn, oats, and soybeans and nearly one-half of the alfalfa and contains about one-third of all livestock, based on value.

There are contrasts within this region, as in the others, and several subregions are recognized because of differences in soils, climate, and type of farming. These five subregions comprise what is often referred to as the Corn Belt. They are: the Central Prairie (*Ia*) in northern Illinois, north-central Iowa, and south-central Minnesota; the Eastern Forest Subregion (*Ib* on the map), consisting mostly of northwestern Ohio and northern Indiana; the Southern Prairie-Forest Subregion (*Ic*) in southern Iowa, northern Missouri, western Illinois, and eastern Kansas; the Western Prairie Subregion (*Id*), mostly in Nebraska and South Dakota and adjacent parts of Minnesota, Iowa, Missouri, and Kansas; and the Northern Forest Subregion (*Ie*) in southern Wisconsin, southern Michigan, and east-central Minnesota.

TABLE 6

Farm Size, Number, Value, and Value Per Acre, North Central States, 1963

Region and State	Number of Farms (1,000)	Land in Farms (1,000 acres)	Average Size of Farms (acres)	Value per Farm $	Value per Acre $
Humid East					
Ohio	140.4	18,507	132	32,583	247
Indiana	128.2	18,613	146	38,489	265
Illinois	154.6	30,327	212	61,946	316
Michigan	111.8	14,782	132	25,535	193
Wisconsin	131.2	21,156	162	21,308	132
Minnesota	145.7	30,796	210	32,605	154
Iowa	174.7	33,830	195	49,150	253
Missouri	168.7	33,155	198	22,094	112
Dry West *					
North Dakota	54.9	41,465	727	38,978	52
South Dakota	55.7	44,850	810	40,852	51
Nebraska	90.5	47,755	530	46,796	89
Kansas	104.3	50,153	480	48,084	100
Montana	28.9	64,081	2,220	76,761	35
Wyoming	9.7	36,200	3,740	79,447	21
Colorado	33.4	38,787	1,150	61,494	53

* Range lands privately owned included in acreage totals.

Source: Bureau of the Census: 1963 revision of 1959 Census.

The Central Prairie Subregion. This region is the Corn Belt *par excellence.* With a total area of approximately 40 million acres, it comprises nearly one-half of Illinois, more than one-half of Iowa, and about one-sixth of Minnesota. The land is level-to-gently-rolling in most of the subregion, and the prairie soils, formed on young glacial drifts, are the most productive in the Midland Feed Region. However, artificial drainage by tile and ditch is required on most fields. Studies by Iowa State University soil scientists reveal that this subregion produced between 12,000 and 16,000 bushels of corn per square mile, or in terms of weight, about 300 to 400 metric tons.[2] Figure 6, showing intensity of corn production, indicates the significance of the Central Prairie Subregion in corn production. This map not only reflects the higher yields of the subregion, but also is an indication of the higher percentage of the land under cultivation.

This subregion still leads all others in percentage of land in corn. Oats were formally the second most important crop in terms of acreage. However, with the increasing tendency of farmers in this area to put the best land in continuous corn and to depend less on rotations in which oats play a major role, oats now rank behind soybeans in total acreage. By 1963, soybean acreage in the Corn Belt states of Ohio, Indiana, Illinois, Iowa, and Missouri had increased to 17.7 million acres, compared to an annual average of 12.1 million acres for the 1951–1960 period. For the same years, oats declined from an average of 12.2 million acres to only 6.5 million acres.

Because of the high percentage of corn and soybeans, the Central Prairie Subregion has 60 percent of its cropland in intertilled crops, compared to only 28 percent for the Northern Forest Subregion. The most intensive grain production is in east-central Illinois and north-central Iowa in what is often referred to as the "Cash Grain

[2] Shrader, W. D., and Riecken, F. F., "Potentials for Increasing Production in the Corn Belt," in Iowa State Univ. Center for Agricultural and Economic Adjustment, *Dynamics of Land Use: Needed Adjustment,* Iowa State Univ. Press, Ames, 1961.

Belt." Here, most grain and soybeans are sold for cash, while in the remainder of the area, a major part of the corn is fed to livestock. In these other areas, hog and beef cattle feeding are major enterprises, utilizing most of the corn on the farm where it is grown. In northeastern Iowa and south-central Minnesota, where there is more hay and pasture land, dairying predominates.

The Eastern Forest Subregion. Topographically, this subregion is very similar to the Central Prairie. However, the natural vegetation was broadleaf deciduous forests and the soils are gray-brown podzolic. They are light in color and low in organic matter except in the extensive areas of poor drainage where organic soils are found. Most of the land is in drainage enterprises, but drainage is still a problem on many farms.

Figure 6 indicates that this subregion is second only to the Central Prairie in the intensity of corn production. Oats are traditionally less important here, however, and wheat becomes the major small grain. Because of the lower natural fertility of the soils, fertilizers and lime have been used for a longer time and in greater quantity than in the western part of the Midland Feed Region. However, corn yields are almost as high as in the Central Prairie Subregion.

The Southern Prairie Forest Subregion. This subregion comprises 36 million acres in south-central Iowa, west-central Illinois, and southeastern Kansas. Less level land is found here than in the two regions discussed above because the older glacial drift plains are more highly dissected by erosion. Most of the level land is in numerous narrow-to-moderately-broad tabular divides with steeply sloping flanks. Tall-grass prairies occupied the divides, but trees were generally found on the slopes and even on the uplands in the eastern part. Loess is the parent material for most of the soils on the divides, and in some areas the clay content is so high as to interfere with subsoil drainage and reduce yields.

Corn is the major crop with soybeans important in the northeastern part of Illinois. Winter wheat is widely grown in the southern part of the area. The livestock-pasture type of farming is increasing, with large farm units often being formed by consolidation of smaller holdings. In Iowa, the largest farms are in Ringgold County, which lies in this subregion and consists mostly of livestock farms. Pasture improvement and conservation practices on the cultivated land, which will be possible on larger farm units, seem to hold the most promise in this subregion.

An interesting comparison between Wayne County, Iowa, in this subregion and Wright County in the Central Prairie Subregion has been made by Wilfrid G. Richards of Drake University. A summary of a part of his findings is given in Table 7. In addition to the data

TABLE 7

A Comparison of Two Iowa Counties

	(S. Prairie Forest) Wayne County	(Central Prairie) Wright County
Approximate land area (acres)	340,480	369,280
Percent of county in farms	93.4	98.2
Number of farms	1,426	1,708
Average size of farms (acres)	222.9	212.4
Cropland harvested (acres)	153,479	396,979
Cropland used only for pasture (acres)	39,093	18,617
Pasture, including woodland pasture (acres)	93,187	16,435
Corn harvested for grain, yields (bushels per acre)	48.8	69.8
Oats harvested, yields (bushels per acre)	20.6	54.4
Soybeans harvested for beans, yields (bushels per acre)	21.6	30.2

Source: U.S. Census of Agriculture, 1959. Compilation by W. G. Richards.

in the table, his study of the county soil surveys indicates markedly lower amounts of total phosphorus, nitrogen, and organic carbon (humus) per acre in Wayne County than in Wright County, and a higher percentage of land in slope.

Western Prairie Subregion. This subregion covers about 60 million acres in Nebraska, South Dakota, and adjacent parts of Iowa, Minnesota, Kansas, and Missouri. It might be called the dry Corn Belt because moisture deficiencies often reduce crop yields. Over 40 percent of the cultivated land is in corn, with yields in the eastern part being more than double those in the west if irrigation is not used. Soils are generally fertile, dark in color, and formed under prairie grasses. In Minnesota and South Dakota they are formed from young glacial materials, while in western Iowa, eastern Nebraska, Kansas, and Missouri they are formed from loess. A large area of sandy soils is found in northern Nebraska.

Because moisture is often in short supply, supplemental irrigation has grown significantly in the last two decades. Most development of irrigation has been in Nebraska along the bottomlands of the Platte and Republican rivers and on the adjacent uplands. There has been considerable development of irrigation of field crops in western Iowa, particularly along the broad Missouri River bottomlands.

Although cropland dominates this subregion, one-third of the area is used for grazing. Livestock, particularly beef cattle and hogs, plays an important role in the farm economy. Also, winter wheat and grain sorghum are grown as cash crops in Nebraska, and in South Dakota and Minnesota, oats, wheat, barley, and flax are important.

The Northern Forest Subregion. This region contains about 52 million acres in southern Wisconsin, southern Michigan, and east-central Minnesota. With cooler climate and shorter growing seasons than the other subregions of the Midland Feed Region, corn is no longer dominant; hay and pasture crops are of prime importance.

Corn occupies only about half of the number of acres that are utilized for hay and pasture crops, and much of that which is grown is cut for silage. Here, the emphasis is on dairying, in contrast to the hogs and beef cattle of the areas farther south. However, dairying is by no means the exclusive type of agricultural land use. General livestock farms are found in most areas, and in southern Michigan near Lake Michigan, fruit farming is important. Also, on many dairy farms hogs furnish an additional source of income, with skim milk, a by-product of cheese and butter manufacturing, constituting an important element in the hog feeding program.

This subregion is often considered separately from the Corn Belt as the Hay and Dairy Region, in combination with the Northern Great Lakes Region and areas in the northeastern United States and southern Canada. However, the relatively high production of livestock feed, particularly for the dairy herds, makes its inclusion in the Midland Feed Region logical. Also, from Figure 6 it can be seen that corn production, in terms of amount per square mile, is of the same order of intensity as in some of the other areas that are more commonly included in the Corn Belt.

Increasing Productivity of the Midland Feed Region. Since the 1930's, food production has continually increased at a rate faster than that of the population growth in the United States. During the 1940's, the annual rate of population growth for the country was 1.5 percent, while in the 1950's it had risen to 1.8 percent. During the same periods, farm output increased at the rates of 2.2 and 2.5 percent per year, respectively. A large share of this increased production has come from farms in the Midland Feed Region. As has been emphasized before, most of this increase has come from increased yields per acre, since total cropland declined some 8 percent in the two decades of the 1940's and 1950's.

Iowa State University agronomists and agricultural economists have been interested in determining the variables that have produced this enviable production record, which has made over-supply, rather than shortage, a problem of American and Corn Belt agriculture. By very carefully removing by statistical analysis the effects of weather fluctuations from the yield picture of major crops, they were able to calculate the increase in productivity that has resulted from crop technology. Four variables were selected that, in addition to weather, have made a pronounced contribution to yields.[3] These variables were (1) crop variety improvement, including hybrids, (2) rates of fertilizer application, (3) regional production location or regional specialization, and (4) all other variables. Most of these variables except weather are the results of crop technology and can be controlled by the farmer.

Table 8 and page 64 summarize the results of the Iowa State University study of the major crops grown in the Midland Feed Region. We see that corn has responded most dramatically of all the crops studied, showing a total increase of 24.5 bushels per acre, or 61.9 percent, between 1939 and 1961, based on estimated "normal" yields. Normal yield is calculated as the yield that would result with a given technology in a normal climatic year, thus eliminating the weather variable from the yield picture. The most significant variable was variety improvement, accounting for an estimated 9.6 bushels per acre increase. Fertilizer application was a close second, accounting for 9.5 bushels. Other technologies, accounting for a 5.4 bushels per acre increase, include such variables as the use of insecticides, herbicides, trace elements, irrigation, drainage, better tillage, and more intensive planting. Of course some of these other technologies, such as planting of higher plant populations, is made possible by fertilizer application, so that there is an interaction among these technologies. For example, increased fertilizer use on corn has resulted, at least in part, from a desire to obtain the full potential of hybrid varieties.

[3] Auer, L. E., Heady, E. O., and Conklin, F., "Influence of 'Crop Technology' on Yields," *Iowa Farm Science,* March, 1966, Vol. 20, No. 9, Iowa State Univ., Ames, pp. 13–16.

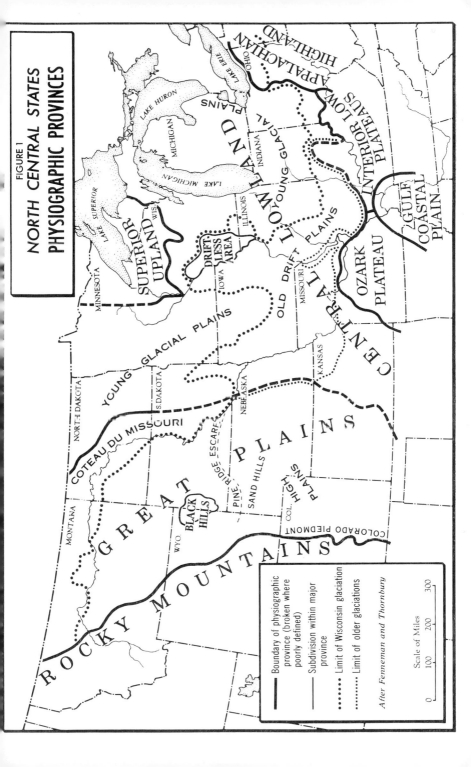

FIGURE 1

NORTH CENTRAL STATES PHYSIOGRAPHIC PROVINCES

Boundary of physiographic province (broken where poorly defined)

Subdivision within major province

Limit of Wisconsin glaciation

Limit of older glaciations

After Fenneman and Thornbury

Scale of Miles

0   100   200   300

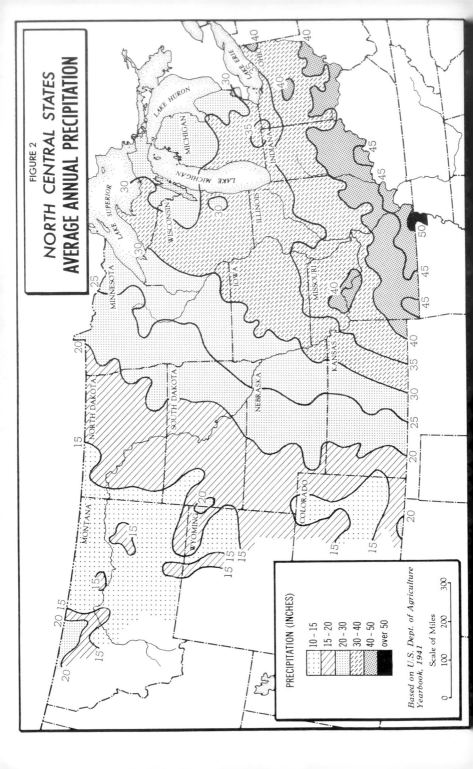

FIGURE 2

NORTH CENTRAL STATES
AVERAGE ANNUAL PRECIPITATION

PRECIPITATION (INCHES)

10 - 15
15 - 20
20 - 30
30 - 40
40 - 50
over 50

Based on U.S. Dept. of Agriculture
Yearbook, 1941

Scale of Miles

0   100   200   300

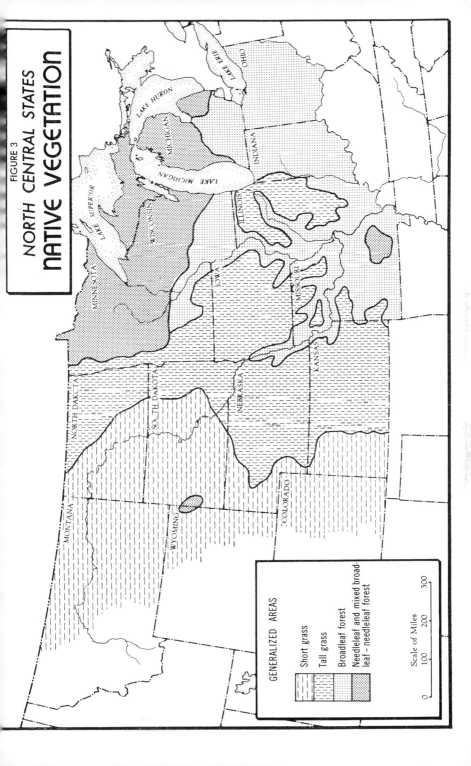

FIGURE 3
NORTH CENTRAL STATES
NATIVE VEGETATION

GENERALIZED AREAS

Short grass
Tall grass
Broadleaf forest
Needleleaf and mixed broad-
leaf - needleleaf forest

Scale of Miles
0   100   200   300

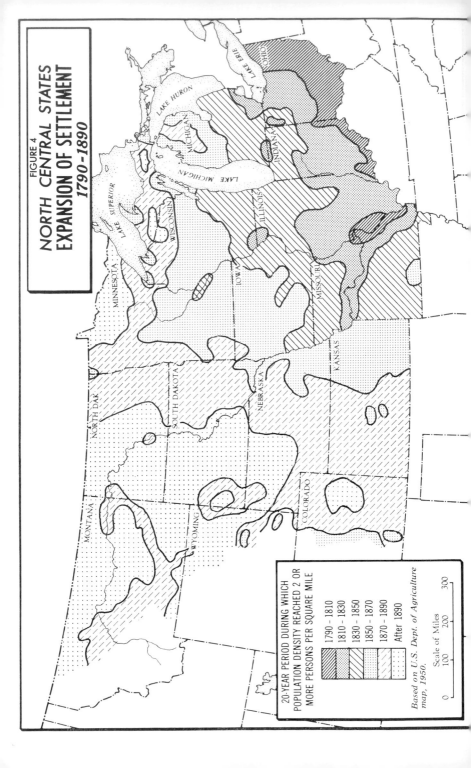

FIGURE 4
NORTH CENTRAL STATES
EXPANSION OF SETTLEMENT
1790-1890

LAKE ERIE

OHIO

LAKE HURON

MICHIGAN

LAKE MICHIGAN

LAKE SUPERIOR

INDIANA

WISCONSIN

ILLINOIS

MINNESOTA

IOWA

MISSOURI

NORTH DAK.

SOUTH DAKOTA

NEBRASKA

KANSAS

MONTANA

WYOMING

COLORADO

20-YEAR PERIOD DURING WHICH
POPULATION DENSITY REACHED 2 OR
MORE PERSONS PER SQUARE MILE

1790 - 1810
1810 - 1830
1830 - 1850
1850 - 1870
1870 - 1890
After 1890

Based on U.S. Dept. of Agriculture
map, 1950.

Scale of Miles

0   100   200   300

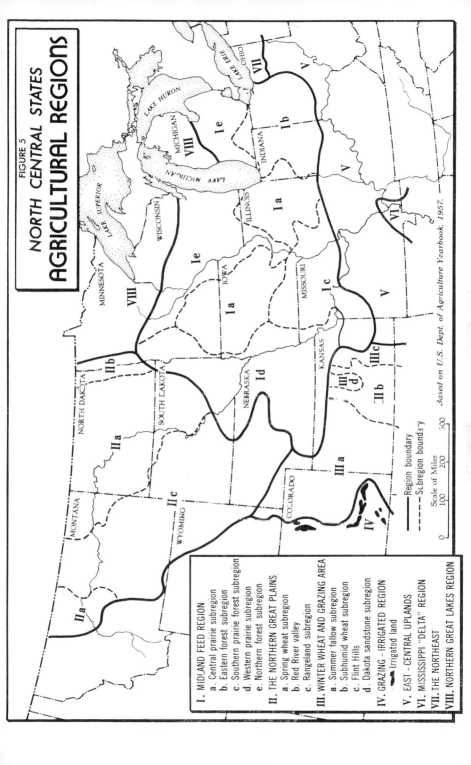

FIGURE 5

NORTH CENTRAL STATES
AGRICULTURAL REGIONS

I. MIDLAND FEED REGION
  a. Central prairie subregion
  b. Eastern forest subregion
  c. Southern prairie forest subregion
  d. Western prairie subregion
  e. Northern forest subregion
II. THE NORTHERN GREAT PLAINS
  a. Spring wheat subregion
  b. Red River valley
  c. Rangeland subregion
III. WINTER WHEAT AND GRAZING AREA
  a. Summer fallow subregion
  b. Subhumid wheat subregion
  c. Flint Hills
  d. Dakota sandstone subregion
IV. GRAZING - IRRIGATED REGION
  ■ Irrigated land
V. EAST - CENTRAL UPLANDS
VI. MISSISSIPPI "DELTA" REGION
VII. THE NORTHEAST
VIII. NORTHERN GREAT LAKES REGION

Region boundary
Subregion boundary

Scale of Miles
0   100   200   300

Based on U.S. Dept. of Agriculture Yearbook, 1957.

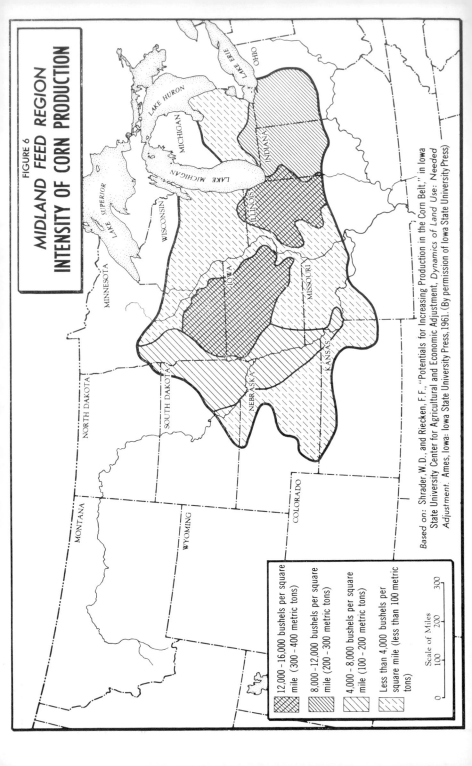

FIGURE 6
**MIDLAND FEED REGION
INTENSITY OF CORN PRODUCTION**

12,000 - 16,000 bushels per square mile (300 - 400 metric tons)

8,000 - 12,000 bushels per square mile (200 - 300 metric tons)

4,000 - 8,000 bushels per square mile (100 - 200 metric tons)

Less than 4,000 bushels per square mile (less than 100 metric tons)

Scale of Miles
0   100   200   300

Based on: Shrader, W. D., and Riecken, F. F., "Potentials for Increasing Production in the Corn Belt," in Iowa State University Center for Agricultural and Economic Adjustment, *Dynamics of Land Use: Needed Adjustment.* Ames, Iowa: Iowa State University Press, 1961. (By permission of Iowa State University Press.)

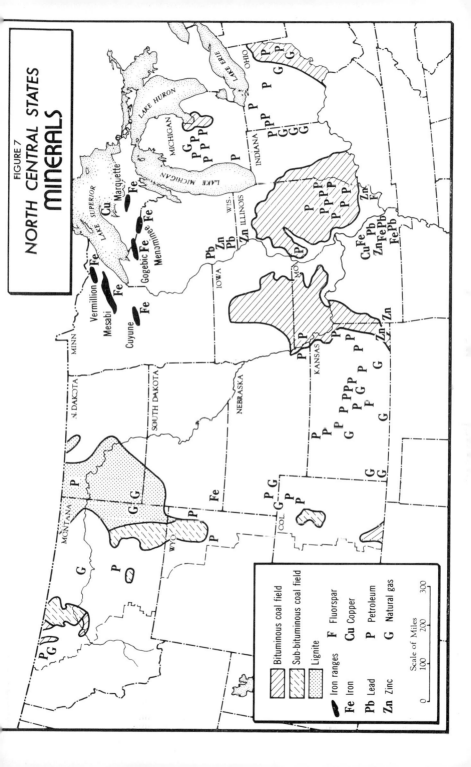

FIGURE 7
NORTH CENTRAL STATES
MINERALS

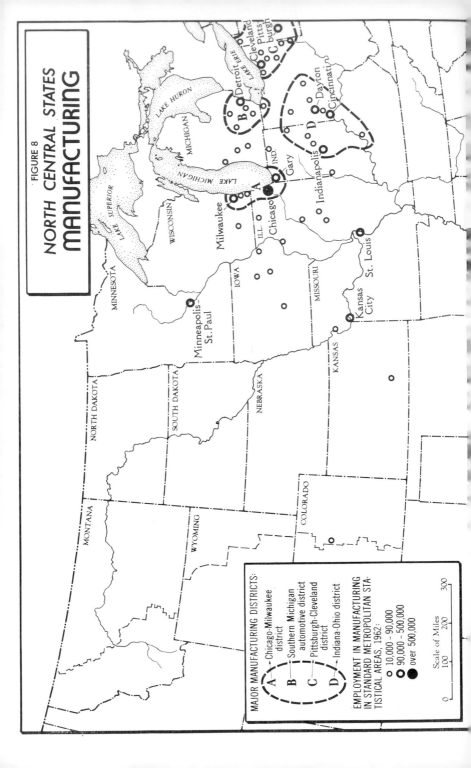

FIGURE 8

NORTH CENTRAL STATES
MANUFACTURING

MAJOR MANUFACTURING DISTRICTS:

A — Chicago-Milwaukee district
B — Southern Michigan automotive district
C — Pittsburgh-Cleveland district
D — Indiana-Ohio district

EMPLOYMENT IN MANUFACTURING IN STANDARD METROPOLITAN STATISTICAL AREAS, 1962:

○ 10,000 - 90,000
◉ 90,000 - 500,000
● over 500,000

Scale of Miles
0   100   200   300

TABLE 8

Estimated contribution of crop yield technologies to acre yields of crops grown in the Corn Belt region, 1939 to 1961. Based on Iowa State University studies

Region and Crop	Time Period	"Normal" Yield in Base Year (bu.)	Yield Changes (bu.)				"Normal" Yield in Final Year (bu.)	Percent Change From Base Period
			Variety Improvement	Fertilizer	Other	Total		
Corn Belt								
Corn	1939–61	39.6	9.6	9.5	5.4	24.5	64.1	61.9
Soybeans	1943–60	19.7	3.0	1.7	0.2	4.9	24.6	24.9
Oats	1942–60	34.5	2.9	2.6	...	5.5	40.0	15.9
Wheat	1939–60	18.8	2.6	4.1	3.0	9.7	28.5	51.6
Iowa								
Corn	1939–61	43.4	...	...	...	20.5	63.9	47.2
Soybeans	1943–60	19.4	...	...	...	4.9	24.3	25.3
Oats	1942–60	37.2	...	...	...	-0.9	36.3	-2.4

Source: Auer, L. E., Heady, E. O., and Conklin, F., "Influences of 'Crop Technology' on Yields," *Iowa Farm Science*, March, 1966, Vol. 20, No. 9, Iowa State Univ., Ames, pp. 13–16.

THE GREAT PLAINS

There are a number of characteristics which set the agriculture of the Great Plains apart from that of most of the other agricultural regions. It is here that the large-scale mechanization of crop production was first carried out, and today this environment is the most favorable for total mechanization of production on an extensive scale. The large, unbroken expanses of level land, low rainfall in the harvest season, and concentration on small grains, particularly wheat, provide a regional setting that is ideal for high production per man-hour involved. The high variability of rainfall results in a considerable increase in the risk involved, with bumper crops in some years and crop failure in others. Average yields per acre are low, although the "average" has little real significance in describing yields on the Great Plains. Variability of yields is highest in a north-south belt lying between areas of lower variability along the moister eastern margins and in the west along the Rocky Mountains where irrigation is more widely practiced. Some counties in northwestern North Dakota, north-central South Dakota, western Kansas, and eastern Colorado had variabilities in wheat yields of over 70 percent during the period from 1926 to 1948. In the more favorable areas to the east and west of the zone of high yield variability, the percentage fluctuation was generally less than 55 percent.

Because of the suitability of wheat for the climatic conditions and the extensive system of agriculture on the Great Plains, this area is the major wheat producing region of the United States. The states in this area account for almost half of the total production, with Kansas, the leading wheat state of the nation, producing some 17 percent of the total. North Dakota is the second most important wheat producing state, accounting for 11 percent of the nation's wheat crop. A summary of the productivity of the Great Plains states in 1964 is given in Table 9. The wheat grown in the Great Plains is of the hard variety having a higher gluten content than soft wheat grown under more humid conditions. The high gluten content makes it more desirable for making bread and thus assures a greater demand and higher market price.

TABLE 9

Wheat Production in the Great Plains Area of the North Central States, 1964

State	Production in 1,000 Bushels	Percent of U.S. Total
North Dakota	150,000	11
South Dakota	37,000	3
Nebraska	73,825	6
Kansas	215,460	17
Montana	90,821	7
Wyoming	5,304	(less than 1 percent)
Colorado	27,664	3
Totals	600,637	47

Source: U.S. Department of Agriculture, Agricultural Statistics, 1965.

The cultivation of grain in the Great Plains has made necessary certain adjustments to the dry climate. Perhaps the most important of these is the practice of *summer fallow*, in which the land is left unplanted, but cultivated, in alternate years. The purpose of summer fallow is to accumulate soil moisture from rainfall during the fallow year and to utilize it subsequently for crops the following year. The fallow land is cultivated to keep weeds from growing and utilizing the moisture. Summer-fallowed land yields more per acre than continuous wheat and is a hedge against drought. Although summer fallowing is not practiced by all wheat farmers on the moister margins of the plains, it is almost universal in the drier areas.

The complete mechanization of grain farming has had a profound effect on the settlement pattern of the plains. Large fields can be cultivated in a relatively short time, the seed can be sown, and there remains little to be done until harvest. If no livestock is kept on a farm, there is little to require the attention of the grain farmer during the growing and maturing of the crop. Thus, large-scale grain farming, in contrast to general farming in the humid east, is a part-time enterprise. This fact has led to a highly mobile farm population. Many farmers have moved into towns and cities to enjoy the amenities of urban life and to work at nonfarm occupations while continuing to farm the land, a situation most prefer to the isolated life on the dispersed farmsteads of this thinly settled land. The farmer who lives in a nearby urban community and commutes to his farm during planting and harvest, often 30 miles or more, is referred to as a "sidewalk" farmer. Others, who may live in faraway cities such as Denver or Kansas City, and who visit the land only to plant and later to harvest, are called "suitcase" farmers. Often the suitcase farmer will own or lease land in widely separated parts of the Great Plains, perhaps in the Winter Wheat Belt of the southern plains and also in the Spring Wheat Belt of the north, thus minimizing the losses he is likely to suffer from climatic disaster in any one area.

Large areas outside the wheat subregions are utilized primarily as rangeland, particularly in eastern Montana, western South Dakota, western Nebraska, and eastern Wyoming and Colorado. Livestock enterprises may be of two types: the stock farm which combines cash-crop agriculture with livestock raising, or the ranch where major emphasis is on livestock. The rancher may also plant some cash crops. The chief difference between these two enterprises, the stock farm and the ranch, is one of emphasis and, as a result, size. The stock farmer depends on cash crops for a major portion of his income, with livestock as a hedge against crop failure. On the other hand, the rancher is principally a livestock man with cash-grain farming a supplementary source of income, or with irrigated forage crops to supplement the natural pastures.

Irrigated agriculture is found along the Colorado Piedmont, the Arkansas River Valley in eastern Colorado and Kansas, and the South Platte River in Nebraska, along parts of the Missouri River in eastern Montana and the Dakotas, and in the Red River Valley of the north. Alfalfa is the most extensively grown irrigated crop and the major one in irrigated acreage from Colorado northward. Potatoes, flax, and corn also are grown in irrigation districts of the Northern Great Plains.

Because of the great north-south extent of the Great Plains, there is enough diversity in climate, topography, and soil, and subsequent land use to justify dividing the area into two agricultural regions and a number of subregions (Figure 5). The Northern Great Plains region contains the well-known Spring Wheat Subregion (*IIa* in Figure 5), the Red River Valley (*IIb*), and the Rangeland Subregion (*IIc*). The Winter Wheat and Grazing Area, lying partly in the southern portion of the Great Plains area within the North Central States, extends beyond into adjacent parts of Oklahoma, Texas, and New Mexico, and contains the Summer Fallow Subregion (*IIIa*), the Subhumid Wheat Subregion (*IIIb*), the Flint Hills (*IIIc*), and the Dakota Sandstone Subregion (*IIId*).

THE NORTHERN GREAT PLAINS

The Northern Great Plains Region includes the Spring Wheat Subregion, the Red River Valley, and the Rangeland Subregion. Rainfall in this region ranges from an annual average of slightly more than 20 inches along the eastern margin, to about 12 inches in central Montana, close to 15 inches in eastern Wyoming, and 15 to 22 inches in the Nebraska Sandhills. Although wheat tends to dominate the cultivated land in the Northern Great Plains, a considerable diversity of crops is found in the more humid eastern section and in the irrigated areas. These crops include alfalfa, sugar beets, potatoes, flax, and corn. Westward from the humid eastern margins and outside the irrigated lands elsewhere, moisture imposes a limit on the variety and acreage of cultivated crops, and wheat becomes almost the sole dry-farmed crop, while grassland for hay and grazing occupies a correspondingly greater area. Throughout the region, steep lands and areas of sandy or thin soils are uncultivated rangeland.

The Spring Wheat Subregion. This subregion extends westward from the Red River Valley to the Rangeland Subregion of eastern Montana and South Dakota, west of the Missouri River. West of the Rangeland Subregion is a noncontiguous part of the Spring Wheat Subregion in north-central Montana bordering the Rocky Mountains. This subregion extends northward across the international boundary into the Prairie Provinces of Canada—Manitoba, Saskatchewan, and Alberta.

The Spring Wheat belt of the North Central States is part of one of the world's major commercial grain farming regions. Supplementary crops include barley, rye, oats, and flax, with corn becoming important in the southernmost part of the subregion. This area produces most of the flax grown in the United States, all of which is used for the production of linseed oil. No flax for linen fiber is grown. A relatively recent development in the area is the increased use of commercial fertilizers. The Department of Agriculture estimates that 80 percent of the soils in the Spring Wheat Subregion are deficient in phosphorus, and nitrogen deficiencies are usually encountered in the moister eastern sections.

The Red River Valley. A subregion of particular interest and uniqueness is the Red River Valley in eastern North Dakota and western Minnesota. The extreme flatness of the valley is due to the fact that it occupies the bed of ancient glacial Lake Agassiz, which was formed when the drainage north to Hudson Bay was blocked by the retreating ice of the last continental glacier. When the ice sheet melted away, the drainage was again opened to the north through Lake Winnipeg, and Lake Agassiz was drained, leaving behind the deep, flat accumulation of lacustrine sediments that form the Red River Valley plain today. These alluvial soils lend themselves to the production of spring wheat, barley, sugar beets, and potatoes. The rainfall here is the most favorable of that of any subregion of the Northern Great Plains, but poor drainage is a problem in wet years—it may cause considerable crop loss and handicaps field operations on the heavier soils.

The Rangeland Subregion. In the Rangeland Subregion of the Northern Great Plains about three-fourths of the area is in native-grass range which is grazed by cattle and sheep. From 5 to 20 percent of the land is cultivated, depending on topography and soils, the chief crop being dry-farmed wheat with some irrigated crops along the major streams. Forage and grain for livestock are the principal crops on irrigated lands, although potatoes, sugar beets, and vegetables are locally important. The Nebraska Sandhills area, consisting chiefly of stabilized old sand dunes with rolling-to-steep slopes, is almost all in rangeland with minor areas along streams utilized for hay and feed crops. Rainfall is higher than in most other areas of the Rangeland Subregion (17 to 23 inches), but it sinks rapidly into the sandy soils, which are of little value for cropping. Ground water is abundant and meets most livestock and domestic needs in the Sandhills.

THE WINTER WHEAT AND GRAZING REGION

The Hard Winter Wheat and Grazing Region of the central Great Plains has more precipitation, longer growing seasons, and milder winters than the Spring Wheat area to the north. Here, the wheat is planted in the fall and harvested early in the following summer. Rainfall varies from 38 inches in the southeast, to less than 14 inches along the western margin. Average moisture conditions are adequate for adapted crops if proper practices are followed; but as in the Northern Great Plains, there is considerable fluctuation in precipitation from year to year, and the threat of drought is always to be reckoned with. Records show that precipitation has been as low as 50 percent of normal and higher than 200 percent of normal in almost all parts of the region, with most stations recording slightly more below-average than above-average years. Higher average temperatures also make the rainfall less efficient than in the cooler Northern Plains. Average length of growing season varies from more than 200 days in southeastern Kansas, to less than 140 days in Wyoming and northeastern Colorado.

There are many similarities between this region and the Spring Wheat area of the Northern Great Plains. The dominance of one crop, the use of dry-farming methods, and extensive, highly mechanized agriculture are found in both areas. However, supplementary crops are somewhat different. In the more humid eastern part, corn plays an important role, and grain sorghums replace corn in the drier western and southern areas. This is the major area for the production of grain sorghum in the United States if that part of the area lying outside the North Central States is included. Kansas leads all states in the long-term average production of sorghum, although Texas leads in acres harvested. Average size of farms is smaller in this region than in the Northern Great Plains, and the area is somewhat more densely populated. In Kansas, the average farm size in 1963 was 480 acres, compared to 727 acres in North Dakota, and 810 acres in South Dakota (Table 6).

Because of differences in climate, soils, and terrain the Winter Wheat and Grazing Region can be divided into four subregions: the Summer Fallow Subregion (*IIIa* in Figure 5), the Subhumid Wheat Subregion (*IIIb*), the Flint Hills (*IIIc*), and the Dakota Sandstone Subregion (*IId*).

The Summer Fallow Subregion. This subregion lies across the boundary between the western part of the subhumid section of the Great Plains and the eastern part of the semiarid section. The eastern boundary follows closely the 25-inch annual average rainfall line that marks the approximate eastern boundary of summer fallowing in this part of the Great Plains. In the eastern part fallowing is used on any particular field only about once in four or five years, while in the western part fields are usually fallowed every other year. Winter wheat is the major crop throughout the subregion, while sorghum, small grains, corn, alfalfa, and hay are supplementary. Narrow bands of irrigated land are found along the Platte, Republican, and Arkansas rivers, with corn, alfalfa, and sugar beets the important crops.

This area contained extensive tracts of grassland prior to World War I, but much of this was put to the plow during and after the two world wars. This reduction of natural grasslands continued until the droughts of the early 1950's and acreage allotments reduced the possibilities of quick profits from wheat production. Today, most of the land suited to cultivation has been plowed, but some relatively large cattle enterprises are found where grassland occurs in large blocks.

The Subhumid Wheat Subregion. This subregion is located in central Kansas and extends southward into Oklahoma east of the Panhandle. This area produces more wheat per acre of total farmland than any other subregion of the Winter Wheat and Grazing Region. Some pasture and rangeland is included but is of secondary importance to cultivated crops. In addition to winter wheat, corn is grown in the northern and eastern parts, and grain sorghum is raised over the whole of the subregion. With the present availability of high-yielding, regionally-adapted hybrid sorghums, this crop has been increasing in acreage. Alfalfa is important on many soil types in the north and east, and on bottomlands throughout the area. However, wheat seems to be the crop best adapted to the subregion, and when acreage allotments were not in effect, it occupied more than twice the acreage of all other cultivated crops combined. In fact, the farmers usually restrict the growing of other crops to the amounts needed to provide feed for their livestock.

The Flint Hills. This is a dissected area in eastern Kansas and northeastern Oklahoma. The Oklahoma section is called the Osage Hills, and the whole region is sometimes referred to as the Bluestem Pastures because of large areas of native tall-grass which have been little altered since settlement. This is the major remnant of tallgrass prairie in the United States. The name Flint Hills derives from the presence of limestone soils which are often filled with flinty rock fragments. However, much of the area in bluestem pastures does not have flinty soils and may have adequate soil depth for intensive cropping.[4]

Although rainfall is high enough for continuous cultivation, the chief utilization of the area since the Civil War has been for fattening beef cattle. The remarkable maintenance of the bluestem pastures in excellent condition after so many years of grazing is due, in large measure, to the leasing arrangements that have been practiced since the 1880's. Cattle have been brought into the area for fattening, and the cattlemen have demanded adequate allowances per animal to promote good gains, thus making overgrazing less likely. Also, most of the animals attain market weight in midsummer, thereby allowing the grasses to make a good growth in late summer. In recent decades there has been a shift to year-round utilization of the range, and some deterioration has been noted. Today, there is a trend away from leasing of pastures for cattle from outside the area, and an increasing emphasis on the production of indigenous beef animals with supplementary feeding of grain in large commercial feed lots.[5]

Although the emphasis of the region is on grazing, there is considerable cultivated land which is often overlooked in descriptions of the area. Nearly one-fifth of the land, usually the deeper soils in the valleys and on some uplands, is cropland. Chief crops grown are wheat, alfalfa, sweet clover, and sorghum. Under good management the yields of wheat are higher than in the wheat areas to the west. Some of the soils have poor internal drainage, and corn does not do well in spite of adequate precipitation, a fact that possibly accounts for the pessimistic evaluation of the capabilities of these soils by the early settlers.

[4] Kollmorgen, W. M., and Simonett, D. S., "Grazing Operations in the Flint Hills-Bluestem Pastures of Chase County, Kansas," *Annals of the Association of American Geographers,* Vol. 55, No. 2, June, 1966, pp. 260–290.
    [5] Federal Reserve Bank of Kansas City, "Grazing in the Bluestem Belt," *Monthly Review,* July–August 1965, Kansas City, Missouri, 1965.

The Dakota Sandstone Subregion. This subregion is just to the west of the Flint Hills in northern Kansas. It is an area of strongly acid soils, low in phosphorus and less fertile than those of the Flint Hills. Originally, they were covered with tall-grass prairies much like those of the Flint Hills, but because of the lower annual rainfall and poorer soils, this region succumbed to overgrazing and does not have the reputation as a grazing area that the bluestem pastures have. About one-third of the area is in native-grass pastures utilized for cattle raising.

In arrangements unlike the leasing arrangements that have characterized cattle production in the Flint Hills, cattle are generally raised locally and kept on pasture until they are shipped to market. Some land is cultivated on most farms to supplement the livestock production. Cultivated lands are subject to erosion by wind and water, and only the reasonably level and deep soils respond well to cultivation. However, more than one-half is cropland, with winter wheat the principal crop. Grain sorghum, hay, small grains, and corn are important. Recently, some irrigation has developed along major streams, with corn as the principal crop.

THE GRAZING-IRRIGATED REGION AND OTHER IRRIGATED AREAS

The Grazing-Irrigated Region extends from the Sierra Nevada-Cascade Ranges on the west to the Great Plains east of the Rocky Mountains. Only that part of the region lying east of the Rocky Mountains is included in the North Central States and is comprised of the Piedmont areas of Montana, Wyoming, and Colorado. This region is topographically a part of the Great Plains to the east, but rainfall is generally less, and agriculture is precarious without irrigation. While rainfall is low within the area, the adjacent Rocky Mountains receive considerably more precipitation, and almost every stream emerging from the mountains has been utilized for irrigation.

Irrigated agriculture is not confined to this region within the North Central States, but also occurs eastward across the Great Plains, particularly along the Arkansas River into western Kansas, the South Platte River in northeastern Colorado, the Platte River in Nebraska, and the Missouri River in eastern Montana, North Dakota, and South Dakota.[6]

The major irrigation scheme on the western Great Plains is the Colorado-Big Thompson Project of northeastern Colorado. Here, the Federal Government has increased the water available by bringing water through a tunnel from the better-watered western slope of the Rocky Mountains. The area served by the Colorado-Big Thompson Project has a population of some 250,000, most of whom are directly or indirectly dependent on agriculture. The cost of the project was vastly greater than the original estimates, but the liability of the farmers has been limited to one-half of the original figure, and the government hopes to pay for the remainder by sale of electricity generated by the project. There has been considerable criticism of the project, and doubt has been expressed as to its economic justification.

Another project to expand irrigated agriculture in the Great Plains region is the Pick-Sloan Plan for multiple-use development of the Missouri River. The project is under joint sponsorship of the U.S. Army Corps of Engineers and the Bureau of Reclamation and was an expedient substitute to forestall the proposed development of a Missouri Valley Authority (MVA) patterned after the highly successful Tennessee Valley Authority (TVA).

THE EAST-CENTRAL UPLANDS

In the western part of the East-Central Uplands agricultural area are the Ozark Uplands, while in the east the area is comprised of the outer margins of the old drift plains, the Interior Low Plateaus, and the unglaciated portion of the Appalachian Uplands. This is

---

[6] Irrigation is carried on to some extent in all of the states of the North Central States. However, in the more humid areas irrigation is supplemental to rainfall and generally is not required for successful farming.

an area of poorer soils and less level land where agricultural development is not so spectacular as in the Midland Feed Region to the north. Here, less than half of the land is cropped and farms tend to be small with an overall average of about 50 acres of cropland each. Many are classified as residential or part-time farms, especially near urban centers and in the mining areas. Corn remains the major crop, with a number of lesser crops raised. Culturally, this area is transitional to the South.

Within the Ozark Subregion there is considerable contrast in agriculture from area to area. In the more rugged and isolated areas, subsistence farmers can still be observed making use of the limited pockets of alluvial land along the streams. However, in some areas such as the Springfield Plateau of southwestern Missouri, a prosperous commercial agriculture has developed with farms reminiscent of the better farm areas of the North Central States. The Springfield Plateau is an important fruit and truck-farming area, producing apples, grapes, tomatoes, and strawberries. Also, an important dairy industry has developed along with poultry raising. Green beans, spinach, and other vegetables are produced for canning. Beef cattle are raised in the Ozark region where large areas of land have been utilized for grazing. Some cattle are fattened locally and move directly to the markets in Kansas City, East St. Louis, and Chicago, while others are shipped into the western Corn Belt for finishing before market.

THE MISSISSIPPI DELTA REGION

This agricultural region is truly a part of the South with respect to climate and agriculture. As has been pointed out, this area is not really a delta in the physiographic sense except at its southern extremity, well outside the North Central States. However, to residents of the region from the mouth of the Mississippi to Cairo, Illinois, the name "Delta" denotes the broad alluvial valley of the Mississippi. This is one of the major cotton-producing areas of the United States and the only part of the Old South that has increased in importance as a cotton producer in the face of the continued westward shift of cotton to the drier areas of the Southwest.

Only the northernmost part of the Delta Region lies within the North Central States—the Bootheel area of southeastern Missouri and the extreme southern tip of Illinois. Missouri produces a little less than 3 percent of the total United States production of cotton, most of which is from this area. Although sizable cotton fields may be seen north of Cairo in Illinois, that state's production amounts to only about 2,000 bales annually, compared with 415,000 bales from Missouri.

In addition to cotton, the most important commercial crop in the Missouri and Illinois parts of the Delta is soybeans. Some winter wheat also is grown. Production of these crops, along with cotton, is highly mechanized, a situation greatly facilitated by the level lands of the floodplain. Many of the farms utilize supplemental irrigation as insurance against drought, and drainage is often a problem during wet years.

THE NORTHEAST

Corresponding to the glaciated part of the Appalachian Highland within the North Central States, this area has less rugged terrain and is considerably more productive than the unglaciated highlands to the south. This area is one of dairying and general farming, with more than half of the land in farms under cultivation. The favorable location in relation to industrial and population centers of the Manufacturing Belt of the Lower Great Lakes is advantageous to dairying. Other crops include corn, wheat, and oats, in addition to the harvested hay crops. An area of special interest is the fruit and truck crops area which occupies the lake plain south of Lake Erie. Here, the tempering effect of the lake has encouraged the production of grapes, apples, peaches, and vegetable crops.

THE NORTHERN GREAT LAKES REGION

This southern extension of the great northern forests includes the area bordering the Upper Great Lakes in the states of Minnesota, Wisconsin, and Michigan. It includes some 50 million acres, much of it cutover woodlands. Farms have an average of only 40 acres of cultivated cropland, with dairying the predominant farm enterprise. Potatoes and fruit are grown on specialized farms. The land is often uneven as the result of heavy glaciation, which resulted in the deposition of sandy, gravelly, stony hills and ridges with many swamps and rock outcrops. Soils tend to be light and acid with low organic content and low fertility. Climate in this area is less favorable than in the regions to the south, with cool summers and short growing seasons.

This area was the scene of very destructive lumbering late in the last century, but today under scientific reforestation and management, the economic productivity of the land is being restored. Forest-related jobs are being created for more than 100,000 full-time and many part-time workers. Many of these workers are part-time farmers, as are many of the workers in the iron and copper mines.

Agriculture in this region is precarious at best. Only about 10 percent of the land is actually farmed, and the cultivated land on most farms is too limited to permit modernization. In addition to the handicap of poor soils and climate, markets are far away. Except for the concentrations of people in the mining centers, this is an empty land, and isolation of the farm population is greater than in almost any other area of the North Central States.

This area was the land of the lumberman and the miner, and agriculture developed as a leftover occupation after the forests were exhausted and after a large part of the mine labor became surplus. In response to the labor demands of the lumber industry and the iron-ore mines, large numbers of Slavs, Scandinavians, Finns, and Cornishmen entered the region, and many of them later turned to farming. Of the immigrants, the Finns have been most successful in making a living from farming in spite of the environmental handicaps. Today, these isolated farmsteads can be identified by the ever-present *sauna* bath houses and the Finnish names on the rural mailboxes and in the rural cemeteries. Perhaps it is the similarity of this environment to the Finnish homeland that has made this adjustment easier for Finns than for other ethnic groups.

5 *Resources of the Land: Minerals* [1]

"Gold is where you find it"—the saying might well apply to other minerals. Unlike the distribution of agricultural resources, which can be explained, in part, by the modern patterns of climate and soils, the distribution of most minerals is the result of geologic events that occurred in past ages. Minerals are distributed unevenly in the North Central States, as they are throughout the world, with some areas richly endowed but others extremely poor in mineral resources. However, location plays a major role in the economics of mineral exploitation. Some minerals of high value per unit of weight, such as gold or copper, are valuable enough to make location with respect to market of relatively minor significance. Others, for example common building materials such as sand and gravel, must be produced near where they are used because low value per ton makes it uneconomical to transport them very far from their sources.

While the exact distribution of mineral resources cannot be deduced from a general knowledge of the geology of the North Central States, some broad generalizations can be made about their location with respect to the geology of the area. In the chapter on the physical setting it was indicated that this part of the North American continent has vast areas of sedimentary rock which con-

[1] Statistical and technical materials in this chapter are based largely on *Mineral Facts and Problems,* Bull. 630, U.S. Bureau of Mines, 1965 edition, Government Printing Office, Washington, D.C., 1965.

tain important mineral-fuel resources such as coal and petroleum. While not all sedimentary rocks contain mineral fuels, all mineral fuels [2] are found in sedimentary rock. Metallic minerals are often, although not exclusively, associated with crystalline rocks of igneous or metamorphic origin; the iron ore of the Superior Uplands is a good example. However, important metallic ores, particularly lead and zinc, also are found in sedimentary rocks. Figure 7 indicates the location of the important minerals of the North Central States. However, some mineral resources, such as the nonmetallic building materials, are so ubiquitous that cartographic representation at this scale is not practical.

The North Central States account for about 20 percent of the total value of minerals produced in the United States. Table 10 indicates the value of all minerals produced by states, the rank among states, the percentage of the national total, and the leading mineral product by value of each state. It is significant that petroleum is the major mineral resource of six states: Illinois, Kansas, Wyoming, Colorado, North Dakota, and Nebraska. Also, South Dakota, which leads the nation in gold production, ranks last among the North Central States in total value of minerals produced, thereby indicating the relatively minor importance of gold in the total picture of mineral production. Also, Missouri ranks relatively low in total value of minerals produced in spite of the fact that it contains the world's major lead district. In fact, lead ranks below cement, stone, and lime in value among Missouri's mineral products.

Although minerals are of vital importance to the economy of the region and to that of the nation as a whole, particularly from a strategic standpoint, the value of minerals produced is far below the value of agricultural products and the value added by manufacturing.[3] Only in Wyoming does the value of minerals exceed

[2] The term "mineral fuels" is here used as synonymous with "fossil fuels" of organic origin. The term thus excludes atomic fuels such as uranium.

[3] Value added by manufacturing is defined as the difference between the value of the manufactured product and the amount expended for raw materials, containers, power, etc. This statistic is considered as a good measure of the magnitude of industrial production.

the value of agricultural products and value added by manufacturing. In North Dakota the value of mineral products exceeds the value added by manufacturing, but is exceeded by the income from agriculture.

TABLE 10

Value of Mineral Products, North Central States, 1964

State	Value ($1,000)	Rank	Percent of U.S. Total	Principal Mineral by Value
Illinois	591,136	8	2.89	Coal
Indiana	211,783	23	1.03	Coal
Iowa	106,630	29	.52	Cement
Kansas	513,269	11	2.51	Petroleum
Michigan	555,495	9	2.71	Iron Ore
Minnesota	497,495	13	2.43	Iron Ore
Missouri	189,305	25	.92	Stone
Nebraska	91,959	31	.45	Petroleum
North Dakota	92,866	30	.45	Petroleum
Ohio	454,937	14	2.22	Coal
South Dakota	52,824	41	.26	Gold
Wisconsin	70,007	37	.34	Sand and Gravel
North Central States *	3,427,706		16.73	
United States	20,471,801		100.00	

* Does not include Colorado, Wyoming, and Montana since the major production of these states is outside North Central States area.
Source: Statistical Abstract of the United States, 1965, p. 704.

The minerals produced in the North Central States can be grouped into the *mineral fuels*—coal, lignite, petroleum, and natural gas; *building materials* such as sand, gravel, cement, stone, clay products, and gypsum; *metallic minerals,* including iron, lead, zinc, and copper; and *chemical raw materials* such as salt, fluorspar, and some limestones. Of these, the mineral fuels are the most valuable, followed by the building materials. As a region, the North Central States leads in the production of iron ore, gold, lead, and fluorspar.

THE MINERAL FUELS

Petroleum and Natural Gas. There are six petroleum-producing provinces wholly or partly within the North Central States. The oldest producing area is the Appalachian province of western Pennsylvania, southeastern Ohio, southwestern New York, West Virginia, and eastern Kentucky. The first well was completed in 1859 at Titusville, Pennsylvania, and later, wells were drilled in Ohio. This field now accounts for less than 1 percent of the national total, but the oil is of high quality with a paraffin base and no sulphur, and produces high-grade lubricants. Toward the end of the nineteenth century and early in the present century, the Indiana-Ohio field was brought into production, but today it is of very minor significance. The Central Michigan field came into production in the 1920's and continues to produce about one-half of 1 percent of the national total. Several small but important fields comprise the Illinois, Indiana, Western Kentucky province, which accounts for about 5 percent of the total United States production, most of which comes from southern Illinois (about 3 percent). The most important field in the United States is the great Mid-Continent province of Texas, Oklahoma, and Kansas. The production from the part of this province that lies in the North Central States amounts to about 5 percent of the national total.

Of the states located wholly within the area, Kansas is the largest producer, with over 106 million barrels in 1964. However, Wyoming was the major producer in that year although part of its production is in the Rocky Mountain field and lies outside the area covered in this book. Six of the ten producing states have shown decreases in production since 1960; while Montana, North Dakota, Ohio, and Wyoming have increased their output.

Natural gas is generally found in some amounts in areas of

petroleum production, with all of the petroleum-producing states having some output of natural gas. Kansas is by far the leading state in natural gas output in the area, and ranks fifth in the nation after Texas, Louisiana, Oklahoma, and New Mexico. An important by-product of some natural gas fields is helium, with Kansas the leading state in output. Natural gas is the most rapidly growing of the fuel-energy resources of the United States. In 1964 the marketed products reached 15.5 trillion cubic feet, a gain of more than 33 percent over the average for the previous decade.

Natural gas is transported from the producing fields to market by pipelines, a vast network of which spreads across the North Central States from the gas fields in the West and South to the consuming areas in the northeastern part of the country. A major problem in gas distribution resulted from the fact that demand varies markedly from season to season with peaks coming during the winter. This fluctuation in demand meant that pipelines had to be constructed to meet peak loads and were not utilized to capacity during the low-demand periods. The problem is being partially solved by storing gas underground at locations between the gas fields and the market. Underground structures similar to those in which natural gas and petroleum are found are utilized, thus, in effect creating artificial gas wells. Gas can be pumped into these underground storage reservoirs during the summer and withdrawn during peak winter demands, thereby making it possible to utilize the pipelines at a much more efficient level.

Petroleum and petroleum products move to market by pipeline, rail, and tanker. In the North Central States, most of the petroleum produced is distributed by pipeline since no seacoasts are present. Some of it moves as crude petroleum which is processed at refineries in eastern market areas such as Chicago and New York, while some is processed in refineries located near the oil fields. There are more than 100 refineries in the North Central States, with Michigan leading in number with 16; while Illinois has 15, Kansas 14, Ohio 11, and Wyoming 10.

Coal and Lignite. In 1918, bituminous coal accounted for 70 percent of the nation's total energy production, and output was 579 million tons in that year. During the depression years of the 1930's production fell to only 310 million tons (1932), but climbed again to the record year of 1947, when it totaled 631 million tons. However, 43 million tons of the 1947 total were exported, principally to Europe to assist in rehabilitation after World War II. By 1961, production had dropped to 402 million tons, but it is now slowly increasing, principally because of the increasing demand for electricity generated by steam plants. By 1952, the share of coal in the energy production of the United States had dropped to 52 percent, and by 1958 it had further declined to only 28 percent.

Coal fields within the North Central States have long been major suppliers for the national market. All states in the area except Michigan, Wisconsin, and Minnesota are important producers, with Illinois, Ohio, and Indiana far ahead of the others. Of the six states that have produced over one billion tons of coal from earliest records to the end of 1964, three are in the North Central States: Illinois (3.8 billion), Ohio (2.2), and Indiana (1?). Pennsylvania leads in total historical production with 8.5 billion tons, but West Virginia has led in annual production in recent years. In 1964, the North Central States accounted for about 26 percent of the bituminous coal and lignite produced in the United States.

Coal varies considerably, generally decreasing in quality from east to west across the North Central States. Coal in the Appalachian field is generally of good quality in terms of energy potential, while most coals of the Great Plains are softer and less efficient as sources of energy. Also, only certain coals will produce coke of a quality suitable for use in blast furnaces for the production of iron and steel. The best coking coals are from the Appalachian field, which extends from Pennsylvania and West Virginia into southeastern Ohio. However, good coking coals are now mined in Illinois and are of great importance to the iron and steel industry in the Chicago-Gary area and to the East St. Louis area. Good coking coals are found in Colorado and are, in part, the basis for the iron and steel industry of the Colorado Piedmont.

Lignite is intermediate between peat and coal. It is sometimes referred to as brown coal and is lower grade than sub-bituminous coal which is found in the same general areas. The bulk of the reserves in the United States are in the northern Great Plains in western North Dakota, northwestern South Dakota, and eastern Montana. North Dakota has 30 of the 35 active mines and 90 percent of the national production. Montana has most of the remaining production. In both states the lignite is used for electrical power generation and residential and industrial heating. Although recoverable reserves are found in 15 states, lignite has not been extensively mined in the United States because of the availability of better quality bituminous coal. It is more widely utilized in Europe, particularly in East Germany, West Germany, and the U.S.S.R.

Most coal is burned to produce heat or power, or is treated to produce metallurgical coke. Since the rapid advent of natural gas for heating homes and the use of diesel locomotives by the railroads, the demand for coal for these purposes has declined. However, the increasing demand for electricity for domestic and industrial use has furnished an expanding market for coal. Today, 82 percent of the electricity used in the United States is thermal in origin, with coal being the major source of heat for operating the steam turbines, although natural gas and lignite are used. Hydroelectric production in the North Central States is of minor importance.

Transportation of coal is chiefly by rail with almost three-fourths leaving the mines by that means. Since coal is a relatively low-cost commodity by weight, almost 74 percent is added to the cost of coal at the mines by transportation. Coal moves on the Mississippi and Ohio rivers and the Great Lakes or by ocean vessels where possible, since water transporation is considerably less expensive than rail or truck. However, railroads are introducing innovations to speed up coal delivery and to reduce the cost of handling and transportation. Some attempts to transport coal mixed with water in pipelines have been made; a 108-mile pipeline is in standby operation between a mine in eastern Ohio and a power plant near Cleveland. As a result of the construction of this pipeline, railroads in the area reduced their rates to be competitive. Technological advances in the long-distance transmission of electricity have made it feasible to build power-generating plants near the source of the coal.

METALLIC MINERALS

Iron Ore. This is by far the most important metallic mineral produced in the North Central States. Several states produce iron ore at present, with Minnesota leading all states of the nation in accounting for 67 percent of the ore. Wisconsin and Michigan add another 10 percent, a total of 77 percent of domestic production coming from the Lake Superior district. Other states producing iron ore in the North Central States are Wyoming, with about 1 percent, and Missouri, South Dakota, and Colorado, each producing less than 1 percent.

Until World War II, the pattern of iron-ore production in the United States had remained relatively unchanged for 75 years, with domestic ores, chiefly from the Lake Superior district, supplying most of the demand. With the end of the war, two significant changes took place in the pattern: first, domestic ores ceased to be the sole major source, and high-grade foreign ores became important; and second, mining of low-grade magnetic taconite was started in the Lake Superior district. Most domestic underground mines have shut down, and open-pit mining has changed from a seasonal to a year-round operation. The preeminence of the Lake Superior district and the Great Lakes transportation system have survived this change.

The use of the low-grade ore called taconite has come about because of the depletion of the high-grade, direct-shipping ores in the Lake Superior area, and the development of technology to enrich these ores through pelletization. The change has been facilitated by altering state laws to give tax incentives to the iron-mining companies to help subsidize the shift. In Minnesota, for example, a constitutional amendment was approved which provided that for the next 25 years taxes assessed against taconite-mining companies would not increase above the general corporate level. As a result of these more favorable tax laws in Minnesota and Michigan, the companies have announced plans to expand taconite plants to a total capacity of some 10 million tons of high-grade pellets annually.

The role of the Great Lakes Waterway in the development of the iron mining and steel industry of the United States cannot be over-emphasized. Most of the iron ore moves from the Lake Superior district to mills at Gary and Cleveland, and to lake ports a relatively short distance from Pittsburgh, by ore carriers on the Great Lakes. At the steel mills the ore is smelted, and iron is produced for the manufacture of steel. More than 93 percent of the ore is smelted in blast furnaces, of which there are a total of 104 in the North Central States, representing 44 percent of the total blast furnaces in the United States. In addition to iron ore, the blast furnace requires coke and limestone in large quantities. Table 11 gives the location of blast furnaces in the area. In addition to the blast furnaces, about 6 percent of the ore is smelted in open-hearth furnaces, while less than 0.2 percent is processed in electric furnaces to produce ferro-alloys. Blast-furnace efficiency has been greatly improved in the past 10 years, chiefly through the use of pellets and other technological improvements.

Copper. Since 1863, with the exception of the depression year of 1934, the United States has been the world's leading producer of copper. Although the major copper-producing areas of the United States lie outside the North Central States, principally in the mountain states of the West, the Keweenaw area of the Upper Peninsula of Michigan is one of the oldest producing areas. Archaeological evidence indicates that copper mining was carried on in prehistoric times on Isle Royal in Lake Superior, where native copper was mined from thousands of shallow pits as early as 3,000 years ago. Although copper had been produced in the American Colonies as

TABLE 11

Location of Iron-Blast Furnaces, North Central States, 1964

Plant Location	Number	Plant Location	Number
Ohio (Youngstown Dist.)		**Illinois**	
Campbell	4	Chicago	20
Hubbard	1	Granite City	2
Warren	1		—
Youngstown	11	Total	22
Total	17		
	—	**Indiana**	
		East Chicago	11
Ohio (Central & South)		Gary	12
Canton	1		—
Jackson	1	Total	23
Massillon	1		—
Middletown	1	**Minnesota**	
New Miami	2	Duluth	2
Portsmouth	2		—
Steubenville	5	Total	2
Total	13		—
	—	**Michigan**	
		Dearborn	3
Ohio (Lake Area)		River Rouge	4
Cleveland	11	Trenton	2
Loraine	5		—
Toledo	2	Total	9
Total	18		—
	—	**Colorado**	
		Pueblo	4
			—
		Total	4
			—
		Total North Central States	108
			—
		Total United States	238
			—

Source: U.S. Department of Interior, *Mineral Facts and Problems, 1965,* Bull. 630, Bureau of Mines, Government Printing Office, Washington, D.C., pp. 457–458.

early as 1709, the discovery in 1840 of the ore deposits in Michigan began a new era of copper production in the United States. In 1964, two states in the North Central States area produced significant quantities of copper: Michigan, 69,040 tons, and Missouri, 2,059 tons, for a total of 71,099 tons. This amounted to about 5.7 percent of the national total. Recent discoveries in the Upper Peninsula of Michigan should eventually increase the production from this area.

Lead. Lead is produced primarily in three separate districts within the North Central States: the southeastern Missouri area; the Tri-State district of southwestern Missouri, southeastern Kansas, and northeastern Oklahoma; and the Galena district of northwestern Illinois and southwestern Wisconsin. In the Tri-State district and the Galena district, lead is found in multiple ores containing zinc and small amounts of silver and copper. The lead ores of southeastern Missouri are relatively pure galena (PbS) with relatively little silver, zinc, copper, or other valuable metals present.

In 1964, four states within the area produced lead, with Missouri, the leading state of the nation, accounting for about 38 percent of the national total of 310,406 tons. Not only is the southeastern Missouri district the richest lead producer of the United States, but it is also the leading lead-mining district of the world. The role of this district probably will increase in importance, since most of the operating companies plan major expansions of mining and smelting capacity. At the Viburnum mine alone, a planned expansion will add 100,000 tons annually to the total; while expansions at Bixby and Bucks, Missouri, will add an additional 100,000 tons by late 1967 or 1968. Expansion of the smelter capacity at Herculaneum, Missouri, is also planned.

Zinc. After iron, aluminum, and copper, zinc is the metal produced and used in largest quantities by industrial countries. The United States has led the world in the production of zinc for the past 50 years with the single exception of 1959 when Canada was in first place. Perhaps no metal produced in the United States has undergone more radical shifts in the areal pattern of production in recent years. During the early 1950's the western states produced about 60 percent of the total, the Tri-State area about 20 percent, and the area east of the Mississippi River about 20 percent. By the early 1960's the areas east of the Mississippi had increased their share of the national production to over 50 percent, while the western states had dropped to 40 percent and the Tri-State district to slightly more than 3 percent. The leading zinc-producing state is now Tennessee, which accounted for 20 percent of the production in 1964.

Within the North Central States two areas are major producers of zinc: the famous Tri-State area where the boundaries of Oklahoma, Kansas, and Missouri meet, and the Driftless Area of northwestern Illinois and southwestern Wisconsin. Since the early 1950's the Tri-State area has declined from its position as the major zinc-mining district to one of relatively minor importance, with only slightly more than 3 percent of the national production in 1964. During the same period, the Driftless Area experienced a modest increase in production and in 1964 accounted for about 7 percent of the total.

The Tri-State district illustrates the effects of changing economic conditions on the production of minerals. Historically, this district has yielded over one-half of the total United States production of zinc and some 30 percent of the world production. In the 1930's this area produced, on the average, about 36 percent of the national total. By the early 1950's, as mentioned above, its share of production had fallen to 20 percent, and by the early 1960's to less than 4 percent. This decline in production reflects the fact that the Tri-State area is a marginal producer with low-grade ores and many small operators. With high zinc prices the area increases production rapidly, while production declines when prices are low. The period since the early 1950's has seen numerous fluctuations in the price of zinc, although the prices in the early 1960's were below those of the early 1950's. Also, increasing labor costs and the lack of modernization by the small mining enterprises has discouraged production. Although production in the Tri-State district is now at a low level, it contains a large share of the known zinc reserves of the United States. In 1964, the Tri-State district produced 18,325 tons of zinc, about two-thirds of which came from Oklahoma, about one-fourth from Kansas, and less than one-tenth from Missouri.

Gold. Gold is undoubtedly the most glamorous of the mineral products of the North Central States, but probably the least significant from the standpoint of the regional economy. We have seen that the major gold-producing state of the nation, South Dakota, is at the bottom of the list of states in total value of mineral production in the area with which we are concerned in this book. However, because of the shortage of gold in the world market and the precarious situation with regard to gold reserves in the United States, this production is important. Consumption of gold for industrial and defense applications has increased in recent years, with about twice the domestic production used in the arts and industry in 1963.

The chief problem in gold production has been the fixed price of the product at $35 per ounce since 1934 in the face of mounting costs of production. The Homestake mine at Lead, South Dakota, is the only large gold mine presently operating in the United States. The second largest producer is the Utah Copper mine at Bingham, Utah, which recovers gold as a by-product of treating copper ore. The Homestake is being mined through three operating shafts on 30 levels ranging in depth from 1,400 to 6,200 feet. It contains more than 200 miles of tunnels or stopes. This mine treated about 1.9 million tons of ore in 1963—about 5,200 tons per day. The Homestake and the Utah Copper mine together produced about 57 percent of the domestic output of gold in 1963. However, due to rising costs of production, the profit margin at the Homestake mine has declined to a low level, which threatens termination of production in the next few years if the decline is not arrested.

NONMETALLIC MINERALS

The nonmetallic minerals produced in the North Central States are chiefly the building materials, including sand and gravel, crushed and dimension stone, clay, and gypsum; and limestone for agricultural and chemical use, salt, and fluorspar. Although the value per weight of these materials is generally relatively low, in the aggregate they almost equal the value of all metals mined in the United States, and they comprise the major mineral product of several states in the region (Table 10).

Sand and Gravel. In terms of tonnage alone, sand and gravel outranks any other mineral product. Deposits are worked in every state within the North Central States, although local shortages may occur, particularly in areas with deep covers of loess such as western Iowa. Mining is by surface excavations and operating units range in size from one-man roadside operations to large corporations with a number of producing plants. The industry is highly mechanized and averages about 65 tons per man-day of operation. The building industry, including the construction of concrete and bituminous paving, accounts for 96 percent of the total consumption of sand and gravel.

Sand is also used for purposes other than cement aggregate. The glass industry requires high-quality sand that meets definite specifications as to size and chemical composition. Large quantities are used by foundries to make molds for casting iron and steel. Other uses for special sands are found in the chemical industry, where they are used as a source for silica, sand blasting, abrasive materials, and filter sands for municipal water plants, and in the manufacture of ceramics.

The glaciated portions of the North Central States are particularly well-endowed with deposits of sand and gravel of glacial origin. Although these deposits are widespread, shortages are developing in the vicinities of many large urban centers, necessitating an increasing cost for transportation, which may be several times the cost of the materials at their source.

Limestone. Limestone is one of the major raw materials produced in the area. Its uses include as cut stone for building purposes, raw material for Portland cement, agricultural limestone, crushed stone for cement and road surfacing, flux for the iron and steel industry, and raw material for the chemical industry. Because of the predominance of sedimentary rocks in the North Central States, many of which are limestones or closely related dolomites, the reserves are widespread throughout the area. Because of the relatively low value by weight of this raw material, production is concentrated near the markets in areas of dense population. Most of the production in the North Central States is east of the Missouri River.

Agricultural limestone is of major importance in maintaining the productivity of the soils in the more humid parts of the country. It is not surprising that over half of the crushed limestone used for agricultural purposes in the United States is produced in the Corn Belt States.

Although only about 3 percent of the stone mined in the United States is used for dimension stone—that is, stone cut into blocks or slabs for construction purposes—several outstanding localities are found in the North Central States. Limestone is the principal dimension stone produced in this area, and in the United States it ranks first in total quantity and third in value after granite and marble. The best known locality is south-central Indiana, where high-quality dimension limestone is produced that can withstand the cost of shipping to distant markets. The Indiana limestone is particularly desirable because of its uniform color and massive structure and the ease with which it can be worked when quarried, although it hardens with exposure to the atmosphere. Another well-known locality which produces particularly attractive limestone is Lannon, Wisconsin.

Gypsum. Gypsum ($CaSO_4 \cdot 2H_2O$) is an important raw material for the construction industry, supplying ingredients for Portland cement, plaster, wall-board, and ceiling tiles. Gypsum is also important as a soil conditioner and as a filler in the manufacture of paper. In 1963, 21 states produced gypsum, with California, accounting for 17 percent of the total production, in first place, followed by Michigan, 13 percent; Iowa, 12 percent; and Texas, 11 percent. Within the North Central States, Indiana, Kansas, and Ohio also produce important amounts of gypsum.

Clay. Clays form another important group of nonmetallic minerals that are produced in large quantity in the North Central States. The principal industrial clays are used for fillers for paper and rubber, cement, and ceramic materials. Large quantities of miscellaneous clays are used in heavy clay products such as brick and tile. The manufacture of tile is particularly widespread in the areas covered by young glacial drifts because of the great demand for drainage tile for agricultural land. Like other low-cost building materials, clay products such as brick and tile are produced as close to market as possible, while some of the special clays may be valuable enough to withstand shipping a considerable distance. Ohio is the leading state in the nation in terms of total tonnage of clay mined, and all of the states in the area have some production.

Salt. Common salt (NaCl) is produced in large quantities in Michigan, Ohio, and Kansas. Two methods of production are used in these areas: (1) underground mining of rock salt; and (2) solution mining, in which water is injected into the salt deposits forming brine, which is pumped to the surface and from which the salt is extracted by evaporation. In addition to the common uses for salt as a seasoning and a preservative, it is used in great quantities in ice removal from streets and highways, and as an important raw material for the chemical industry.

Fluorspar. This is another mineral product in which the North Central States leads the nation, chiefly because of the production from the Illinois-Kentucky district. Until recently, the major use of fluorspar (CaF_2), which is the mineral fluorite in the pure form, was as a flux in the manufacture of steel in the basic open-hearth, basic electric furnace, Bessemer converter, and basic oxygen steel furnace. However, in the last few years the major consumption of fluorspar has been in the manufacture of hydrofluoric acid, a widely-used raw material for the chemical industry. Some is also used in the manufacture of certain ceramic products; and small quantities of clear, flawless crystalline fluorite are used for lenses and prisms in optical equipment. The great fluorspar mining district of southern Illinois and western Kentucky produced almost 84 percent of the nation's total of fluorspar in 1963, with Illinois being the major producer with 80 percent of the district's total. Lead and zinc are important by-products of fluorspar mining in the Illinois-Kentucky field and are important economic factors in the mining operations.

MINING COMMUNITIES

Mining settlements have a reputation for instability stemming from the "boom-or-bust" economy often associated with the exploitation of minerals. The mining communities of some parts of the North Central States are no exception. In addition to overdependence on a single resource, many of the mining centers are located in areas of limited agricultural potential, thereby adding to the difficulty of shifting to another economic base. The iron-mining centers of the Superior Upland and the coal-mining communities of southern Illinois offer good examples of the problems inherent in many mining areas.

Hibbing, Minnesota, at the site of the famous Hull-Rust mine on the Mesabi Range, has not suffered as much as some other mining communities from the undesirable side effects of mining. Part of this more fortunate situation stems from the tax laws of Minnesota, which have permitted heavy taxation of the iron-ore reserve as well as the ore production. Most of this tax money has been poured back into the mining communities, which accounts for the fine schools, excellent municipal facilities, and good streets and highways. The state had learned well its lesson from the destructive logging era, during which vast wealth was removed from the area, leaving a wasteland behind. Today, these tax laws have been revised to encourage the mining companies to expand their taconite-processing facilities in order to stem what had seemed to be an inevitable decline in iron-ore production.

With the exhaustion of high-grade hematite ores, the area underwent a gradual decline, and Hibbing, along with other mining communities, suffered a loss of population between 1940 and 1950. However, there was a small increase in the decade 1950–1960, and further growth now seems assured as mining again expands with the exploitation of the taconite ores. The shift of the mining population into agriculture, both full- and part-time, has been discussed in the preceding chapter.

The situation in the coal-mining communities of southern Illinois parallels to some degree that of the iron-mining areas of the Upper Great Lakes. However, there are some striking differences between the two areas. No special tax laws exist in Illinois to assure a share of the profits for the coal-mining towns. Although great wealth has been taken from the earth, the area has been one of chronic economic depression. With the decline in demand for coal and the parallel introduction of mechanized operations, the jobs in mining decreased. Also, this trend was furthered by the shift from shaft to strip mining, which requires less labor. Although the miner in southern Illinois is one of the best paid laborers, the jobs are few. There has been a reluctance among the unemployed miners to leave the area because the hope for high-paying jobs in mining is always present.

The late Charles C. Colby summarized the situation in southern Illinois as follows:

Probably the coal miners make more in the coal mines than in any other line of work open to them. If this be the case, they are not likely to move. Unemployed miners remain in the area in the hope of finding a job in the mines, even though there is little or no hope of such an outcome. The lot of the employed miners has improved, whereas that of the unemployed has become tragic.[4]

The reluctance of the southern Illinois miners to leave the area has been bolstered by the fact that many of them own their own homes and often a small farm. Although the lands of the mining counties are generally of poor quality, they are farmed at what amounts to a subsistence level. Thus, the farm is an insurance policy against the periods of unemployment and can assure the family of a minimal living, a situation which the former miners are reluctant to abandon.

[4] Colby, Charles C., *Pilot Study of Southern Illinois,* Southern Illinois Univ. Press, Carbondale, 1956, p. 42.

6 *Resources of the Land: Forests and Forest Products*

Prior to European settlement of North America, the North Central States contained one of the world's great expanses of middle-latitude forests. Magnificent trees covered the land from the Appalachians westward to the prairie grasslands and extended in long fingers up the river valleys and into the rougher lands of the grassland areas. In the Lake States [1] of Michigan, Wisconsin, and Minnesota the transition from broadleaf deciduous forests to taiga gives rise to a mixed forest, which was intact long after the deciduous forests to the south and east had been largely replaced by agriculture. However, the forests of Ohio, Indiana, southern Illinois, eastern Iowa, and southern Missouri were barriers to settlement, and where they occupied good, level land they were removed rapidly to make way for cultivation. In the clearing process, the forests supplied raw materials for house construction and fuel, the log cabin and rail fence being the symbols of the frontier.

Commercial exploitation of the forest resources for lumber centered chiefly in the Lake States, and developed rapidly in the last half of the nineteenth century in response to the growing demands

---

[1] The Forest Service divides the North Central States into several statistical region: *the Lake States*—Michigan, Wisconsin, and Minnesota; *the Central States*—Ohio, Indiana, Illinois, Iowa, Missouri, and Kentucky; and *the Plains States*—North Dakota, South Dakota, Nebraska, Kansas, Oklahoma, and central and western Texas. All of these divisions, with the exception of the Lake States, extend beyond the boundaries of the North Central States.

of the expanding urban-industrial complex of the northeastern United States. The most prized tree was the northern white pine (*Pinus strobus L.*), but large stands of northern hardwoods such as beech, birch, and maple were also present. With the rising demand for lumber for building construction and the depletion of the white pine forests of the Northeast, lumbermen moved westward, first to Michigan, which became the leading lumber state in 1870, then to Wisconsin, and, later, to Minnesota. By 1910, the great forest resources of the Lake States were all but gone, and the production was not sufficient to meet local needs for lumber.

The record of lumbering in the Lake States is a black mark on the nation's record because of wasteful utilization of natural resources. The destructive methods of logging left a wasteland that has not yet fully recovered. The land was cutover and abandoned to weed trees and subsequent forest fires, many of which not only destroyed the young trees and damaged the soil, but also caused the destruction of towns and the loss of human life. Today, where soils are not suitable for agriculture, thousands of square miles of scrubby second growth cover the landscape, and reforestation has proven difficult. The term "Cutover Area" is often used to designate the formerly forested lands of the Lake States. Here, we have forest exploitation more comparable to the mining of a natural resource, in contrast to the treatment of forests as a renewable resource. Fortunately, the lesson learned in the Lake States has resulted in a more rational approach to forest management to assure a continued supply of wood through tree-farming rather than "mining" the forest.

After the initial clearing for agricultural settlement, lumbering never dominated the forest areas to the south of the Lake States. Local saw-milling enterprises were developed but were secondary to agriculture. Even in rough areas where forest lands still occupy large acreages, the lumbering was never on the scale that developed in the Lake States. With the spread of agriculture the forests remained only in farm woodlots, wooded pastures on poor soils or rough topography, or in the rather extensive areas of hilly terrain in the Interior Low Plateaus, the Appalachian Plateaus, and the Ozarks.

FOREST-RELATED INDUSTRIES

Today, forest industries are still important in the Lake States and in other areas in the eastern part of the North Central States. Only on the central Great Plains are forest industries almost entirely absent. However, the total area now accounts for only about 9 percent of the total volume of timber cut for all uses in the United States, with about 56 percent of this cut originating in the Lake States. Where once white pine was the principal lumber-producing tree, hardwoods now account for 80 percent of the cut in the North Central States as a whole, and 65 percent in the Lake States. In contrast, the South accounts for about 47 percent of the total national cut, and the West, 35 percent of the total. If only sawtimber, used for producing lumber for construction purposes, is considered, the North Central States rank even lower, accounting for only 7 percent of the board-feet produced. This reflects the importance of nonlumber products, primarily pulp.

Forest-related industries in the North Central States include lumber milling, pulp and papermaking, production of cooperage (barrel staves and heads), the manufacture of charcoal, and the production of mine props and railroad ties. Each of these industries has a characteristic distribution pattern in the area, depending on its unique relationship to the sources of raw materials, transportation, and markets.

The Lumber Industry. Lumber mills are generally located near the source of raw materials because logs are difficult to transport and have a low value per unit of weight, and because about half of the volume of a log is lost as sawdust, slabs, and bark. Consequently, the distribution of lumber mills is very similar to that of the remaining stands of forest. The larger mills are concentrated chiefly in the Lakes States, particularly in northern Wisconsin, and the smaller units in the remainder of the area east of the Missouri River. Although a few mills are present on the eastern and western margins of the Great Plains, they are almost entirely absent on the central plains. The larger mills, again in the Lake States, maintain logging camps to supply their needs, while the smaller mills usually depend on the purchase of timber from wood lots, the cutting being done by small logging crews or by the farmers themselves. Larger mills may depend heavily on streams and lakes for floating logs to the mills, while smaller mills outside the Lake States are primarily serviced by trucks.

An important factor in the economics of lumber-mill operations in the North Central States is the advantage of being close to the major markets for lumber in the industrial areas of the Northeast. Many small mills are able to operate at relatively low levels of efficiency because of what is in effect a subsidy due to location. A study by Iowa State University of the source of lumber used in Johnson County in the eastern part of Iowa, indicated that 60 percent of all lumber used on farms in the county was native lumber sawed by local mills.[2] Although operation of these mills is substandard and the quality of product highly variable, they have competed successfully for the market for lower grades of lumber in the local area. This has been possible because increased freight rates from the West Coast and the Deep South, which now often equal or exceed the initial cost of low grades of lumber, have worked to the advantage of the Iowa lumbermen by guaranteeing a minimum price and placing the native product in a favorable position to compete with imported lumber. This situation undoubtedly exists in other areas of the North Central States.

Pulp and Paper Manufacturing. Most pulp mills depend on sources of soft wood, principally conifers and softer broadleaf trees

[2] Iowa State College, Agricultural Extension Service, *Sawmills in Iowa,* Ames, 1953.

such as poplar, and the distribution of the mills is partly explained
by the availability of these trees. In the North Central States the
major concentration of mills is in the Lake States, where the small
second-growth trees of the cutover area assure a supply of pulp
wood. A few mills are located in eastern Ohio near the Appalachian
uplands. Because of the small size of trees required, the planting
of trees on abandoned lands will return a profit to the farmer in a
relatively short time, thus providing a source of income to agriculture in an area that tends to be submarginal. Also, some paper
companies have established tree farms in these areas to assure a
continuing supply.

Pulp manufacturing also requires large supplies of water and
power to operate the pulping machinery. Because of the noxious
quality of the chemical waste from pulp mills, the problem of
stream pollution has become acute in many of the areas. Also,
certain types of pulp processes create a problem of air pollution due
to the obnoxious odors produced.

Paper and paper products are closely related to the production
of wood pulp. Some paper mills are located near the source of wood
pulp and may even be a part of an integrated plant where paper
is the final product. Others are located in the large metropolitan
areas such as Chicago and transport the raw materials from the
pulp mills. Most paper and paper products use not only wood pulp,
but other raw materials such as rags, waste paper, and cotton lint.
However, newsprint and wrapping papers are made almost exclusively from pulp and therefore tend to locate near the raw
materials. Within the North Central States, Chicago is by far the
major single center for the manufacture of paper and paper
products.

Furniture Manufacturing. The furniture industry of the United
States is largely concentrated in the northeastern part of the country
and closely follows the pattern of population concentration. Chicago
is second, after New York, as a center for the manufacture of

furniture. Although forests supply a major share of the raw materials, furniture manufacturing is not oriented to the raw materials. Much of the wood used is imported from areas outside the region from as far away as the tropics, thus reflecting the relatively high value added by manufacturing in the industry. There is some demand for hardwoods from the North Central States, particularly oak, gum, and walnut. However, it has proved difficult to interest the landholders of small, private woodlands in investing in planting and proper management.

The Future of Forest-Products Industries. Although forests are making a modest comeback in the Lake States and other areas, the process of increasing forest production is a slow one. The Forest Service estimates that about one million acres of trees have been planted in the Central States area in recent decades, but an estimated 7 million acres are still in need of planting. A high proportion of the forest and potential forest land is in small, privately owned plots, which makes it difficult to obtain wide acceptance of good forest management. It would seem desirable to expand planting, not only to add to our commercial forest resources, but to restore idle land to productivity, to control erosion, to establish windbreaks, and to develop areas for recreation and wildlife habitat.

7   *The Processing and Distribution of Commodities*

IN the chapters on agriculture, mining, and forestry, the products of the land were emphasized. Equally important in a modern industrial nation is the processing of these resources into finished products for the consumers by manufacturing. Some types of manufacturing were discussed in the previous chapters, chiefly those which utilize directly the products of mining and forestry, such as the primary iron and steel industry, the building-materials industry, and the wood-products industries. In this chapter we shall be more concerned with the concentration of manufacturing establishments in manufacturing centers and manufacturing districts. Closely related to manufacturing is the transport system that delivers the raw materials to the manufacturing plants and carries the finished products to market.

MANUFACTURING

Location of Manufacturing. There is a close relationship between density of population and the concentration of manufacturing in the North Central States. This is not surprising since labor is one of the chief requirements for the establishment of a manufacturing center. Dense population also means a large market for the manufactured products. Although the availability of raw materials is important in all industries, only a few are strictly raw-material oriented. We have indicated some of these in previous chapters; for example, the low-cost building-materials industries and some wood-products industries. Most manufacturing establishments use processed raw materials obtained from primary industries in the vicinity, or raw materials that can stand the cost of shipping from a considerable distance. An example of the first category is the automobile industry, which depends on the primary-metals industry in the eastern part of the North Central States to supply the raw materials for construction of vehicles. An example of the second is the rubber industry, which imports natural rubber from halfway around the globe.

In the North Central States the greatest concentration of manufacturing is in the states east of the Mississippi River and south of the Great Lakes. In the sparsely settled western part, large concentrations of manufacturing are absent except in a few scattered places such as the Colorado Piedmont. Unlike agriculture, industry does not occupy a continuum of land surface, and even in areas of greatest concentration, manufacturing centers may be surrounded by agricultural land. On a recent trip across the heart of the Southern Michigan Automotive District on Interstate Highway 94, the writer was impressed with the rural nature of the landscape. From the fruit farms in the vicinity of Benton Harbor, to the dairy and general farms in the vicinity of Kalamazoo, Jackson, and Ann Arbor, manufacturing establishments did not dominate the landscape except near the larger cities. After leaving the great concentration of manufacturing around the southern end of Lake Michigan in the Chicago-Gary area, it was not until reaching the vicinity of Detroit that one found manufacturing again intruding itself into the landscape to any great degree.

The concentration of manufacturing in the eastern part of the North Central States is included in the American Manufacturing Region that extends from the vicinity of the Mississippi River in the west, to the Atlantic Seaboard in the east. Geographers differ as to the boundaries of this region, especially on the western margin, because of the discontinuous nature of manufacturing in an areal sense. Instead of an attempt to delineate exactly the extent of the

Manufacturing Region, several manufacturing districts have been indicated in Figure 8, and centers with 10,000 or more employees in manufacturing have been mapped. The Bureau of the Census reports statistics for groups of states that are designated as Census Regions. Two of these Census Regions comprise a major portion of the North Central States, and the eastern margins of a third make up the western extremity of the area. Included are the East North Central, made up of the states of the North Central States area lying east of the Mississippi River; the West North Central, made up of all of the remaining states of the region that are located entirely within the North Central States; and the Mountain States, only the eastern margin of that region having been included in our area. The states included by the Bureau of the Census in these and other Census Regions of the United States are listed in the footnote to Table 12.

In Table 12, a comparison is made between the Census Regions of the North Central States and the other Census Regions of the country for the years 1958 and 1963, in terms of the number of employees in manufacturing, the total value added by manufacturing, the percentage change between the two years, and the 1963 percentage of the total national value added by manufacturing for each region. These statistics reveal that the East North Central Region, made up of Ohio, Michigan, Indiana, Illinois, and Wisconsin, leads the nation in number of employees in manufacturing and in value added by manufacturing, and accounts for a little more than 29 percent of the total value added for the United States as a whole.

In the decade prior to 1958, the American Manufacturing Region showed a loss in industrial employees and seemed to be declining with respect to other Census Regions. Industrial growth was spectacular in the South and Southwest, and continued relative decline of the old centers of manufacturing was foreseen by some observers. However, the half decade 1958–1963 showed an increase in the Manufacturing Region's share of the national total value added by

TABLE 12. Summary of Manufacturing in the North Central States and the United States by Census Regions, 1958–1963.

Census Region [1]	Employees in Manufacturing				Value Added by Manufacturing				Percent of United States Value Added	
	1958 (1,000)	1963 (1,000)	Total Change (1,000)	Percent Change	1958 (Mil. $)	1963 (Mil. $)	Total Change (Mil. $)	Percent Change	1958	1963
East North Central	4,256	4,480	224	+ 5.2	40,691	55,699	15,008	+37	28.0	29.2
West North Central	964	1,024	60	+ 6.2	8,593	11,811	3,218	+37	6.1	6.2
Mountain [2]	104	121	17	+16.5	1,014	1,448	434	+42	0.7	0.8
Total North Cent. States	5,324	5,625	301	+ 5.7	50,298	68,959	18,661	+37	35.6	36.2
New England	1,309	1,432	123	+ 9.5	10,446	13,397	2,921	+28	8.0	7.0
Middle Atlantic	4,152	4,117	−35	− 0.8	35,045	43,463	8,418	+24	23.8	21.9
South Atlantic	1,894	2,148	254	+13.4	14,276	20,527	6,305	+44	10.3	10.9
East South Central	783	892	109	+13.9	6,357	9,041	2,684	+43	4.5	4.8
West South Central	798	860	62	+ 7.8	7,748	10,656	2,908	+37	5.5	5.7
Mountain [3]	235	285	50	+21.2	2,300	3,382	1,082	+47	1.6	1.8
Pacific	1,565	1,683	118	+ 7.5	15,260	22,379	6,758	+45	10.7	11.7
Total United States	16,047	17,065	1,018	+ 6.3	140,706	190,395	49,689	+35	100.0	100.0

[1] Census Regions: East North Central—Ohio, Ind., Ill., Mich., Wis.; West North Central—Minn, Iowa, Mo., N.D., S.D., Neb., Kan.; Mountain—Mont., Idaho, Wyo., Colo., N.M., Ariz., Utah, Nev.; New England—Maine, N.H., Vt., Mass., R.I., Conn.; Middle Atlantic—N.Y., N.J., Pa.; South Atlantic—Del., Md., D.C., Va., N.C., S.C., Ga., Fla.; East South Central—Ky., Tenn., Ala., Miss.; West South Central—Ark., La., Okla., Tex.; Pacific—Wash., Ore., Cal., Alaska, Hawaii.

[2] Includes only states in North Central States.   [3] Includes states as in footnote 1.

Source: U.S. Bureau of Census, Census of Manufactures, 1958, and Annual Survey of Manufacturing, 1963.

manufacturing. The rate of growth based on the percentage increases between 1958 and 1963 was less spectacular than that for the South and West; but with a larger base from which to start, the absolute increase was vastly greater. The smaller percentage increase in employees in manufacturing, compared with the increase in value added, is indicative of greater efficiency in manufacturing and greater productivity per man-hour of labor. These statistics also show that the major share of the growth of the old Manufacturing Region has taken place in the North Central States, while the Middle Atlantic portion has increased more slowly in total value added and has shown a slight loss in total employees in manufacturing. Of the North Central States, Michigan showed the greatest percentage growth in value added between 1958 and 1963 with a total increase of 57 percent.

Not only is there a contrast in the intensity of manufacturing between the eastern part of the area, represented by the East North Central Census Region, and the western part, represented by the West North Central Region and the eastern margin of the Mountain Region, but there also is a contrast in the type of manufacturing. In the East North Central Region, machinery and transportation-equipment manufacturing are in first and second place, with primary metals ranking third. The importance of transport equipment reflects the concentration of the automobile industry in this area, and the high rank of primary metals results from the concentration of iron and steel plants along the lower Great Lakes. In the states west of the Mississippi River, food processing leads all industries, with transport equipment and machinery ranking second and third. This suggests the importance of processing agricultural products and the manufacturing of farm equipment.

THE MANUFACTURING DISTRICTS

Four major manufacturing districts are generally recognized in the North Central States: (1) the Pittsburgh-Cleveland District, the western part of which is in Ohio; (2) the Southern Michigan Automotive District; (3) the Chicago-Milwaukee District; and

(4) the Indiana-Ohio District (see Figure 8). In addition, there are several major manufacturing centers lying outside the four districts: namely, Minneapolis-St. Paul, St. Louis, and Kansas City. A number of lesser manufacturing centers are indicated on Figure 10, some located within the major districts and some without.

The Pittsburgh-Cleveland District. The western part of this greatest of all North American iron and steel producing districts lies within the North Central States in eastern Ohio. This section of the district includes the major steel centers of Youngstown, Steubenville, and Loraine, as well as Cleveland. The great concentration of iron-blast furnaces within this region can be seen in Table 11. Not only is this a major area of iron and steel production, but it is also an area of one of the major concentrations of metal-working industries in the country. Although the metals industries dominate the district, many other types of manufacturing are carried on. Of particular significance to the automobile industry are the manufacture of rubber products, which is centered in Akron, Ohio, and the clay-products industry and the glass industry. Of special importance among the metal-working industries is the machine-tool industry, which produce tools and machines to equip other manufacturing establishments.

This district is well-located for heavy industry. The Great Lakes Waterway furnishes cheap transportation of iron ore from the iron ranges of the Lake Superior region, and excellent coking coal is close at hand in the Appalachian coal fields. Semifinished steel products find a ready market in industries within the district and in the major industrial areas of the Midwest and the Mid-Atlantic states. The transportation network is excellent for the distribution of manufactured products since all major east-west railroads and highways from the Mid-Atlantic Seaboard to the Midwest pass through the district. It is also well-served by major pipelines from both west and east. Although the Pittsburgh-Cleveland District has met competition from the Chicago area and from the Tide-Water iron and steel industry in eastern Pennsylvania and Maryland, it has continued to increase its importance.

The Southern Michigan Automotive District. The focus of this district is on the "Automobile Capital of the World," Detroit. Although automobile assembly is highly concentrated in the Detroit metropolitan area and in a ring of adjacent cities, many of the components are made in numerous smaller centers in Michigan and adjacent parts of Ohio and Indiana. In recent decades there has been some decentralization of the automobile industry to take advantage of assembly of the finished product nearer to the markets. However, the Southern Michigan Automotive District still accounts for a major share of the production, and the North Central States area as a whole has about three-fourths of the nation's workers who are engaged in making motor vehicles and parts.

A number of geographic and nongeographic factors resulted in the eventual emergence of the Southern Michigan area and Detroit as the main center of automobile production in spite of the fact that the early industry was also important in New England. When the automobile industry was in its infancy, the construction of horse-drawn carriages was a major industry in the area, and the reservoir of skilled carriage makers was available to produce the gasoline-powered "horseless carriages" which so closely resembled the horse-drawn variety. Also, the presence of level terrain was a boon to the low-powered vehicles, which had difficulty negotiating steep hills such as might be encountered in New England. The strategic location with reference to the iron and steel industry of the lower Great Lakes and the Pittsburgh area, and the rubber industry of Akron, gave easy access to needed materials. The machine-tool industry provided a pool of skilled labor as well as suppliers for equipping the automotive plants with the needed machinery to produce engines and other parts. Also, the well-paid laborers of the area provided a ready market for the automobiles. The fact that Detroit became the center of the industry rather than other equally favorably located cities such as Cleveland, probably resulted from the presence of such pioneers of the industry as Henry Ford, who produced the first automobile cheap enough to sell to a mass market through the use of mass-production techniques.

Today, the automobile industry makes this district the most highly industrialized area of the country in terms of the percentage of the labor force engaged in manufacturing. Detroit is the major steel-consuming center of the United States, but it ranks only fifth as a steel-making center. Although decentralization of the automotive industry is increasing and the Southern Michigan Automotive District will undoubtedly produce a smaller percentage of the total in the future, it seems destined to remain the major center for the industry for some time to come.

The Chicago-Milwaukee District. This district is located around the southern and southwestern shores of Lake Michigan, extending from the northwestern corner of Indiana to the Milwaukee metropolitan area. Industry is highly diversified in the district, ranging from the heavy primary metals industries of the Gary-South Chicago area, to the machinery and machine-tool industries of Milwaukee.

Large quantities of the materials used in the diversified industries within the district are produced by the steel mills and other primary-metals industries in the zone of heavy industry that is concentrated between South Chicago and Gary. Here is one of the great concentrations of heavy industry in the world, as is evidenced by the miles of steel mills along the Lake Michigan shoreline. Rising above the flat lake plain, the rows of blast furnaces and chimneys dominate the landscape as in no other industrial area the writer has observed.

The industry of Chicago itself is more diversified, although metals products lead all other types of manufacturing. According to the last Census of Manufactures, electrical machinery, primary metals, fabricated metals, and machinery rank in that order. However, a host of other types of manufacturing plants are found in the Chicago metropolitan area, including food processing, printing, paper products, chemicals, furniture, and many others. All of these contributed to making Chicago the second manufacturing center of the United States after New York.

Petroleum refining is also of major importance in the Chicago metropolitan area. Most of the refineries are in the vicinity of South Chicago and Whiting, where one of the major concentrations of the nation is located. This is a market-oriented operation. With no local supplies of crude petroleum, the raw material must be brought in from oil fields from the southwest, principally in Oklahoma and Texas. In close association with the refineries is the important petrochemical industry.

The Milwaukee metropolitan area is second in importance to Chicago as a manufacturing center in the district. It is one of the major producing areas for machine tools and engines. With its advantageous location in the nation's major agricultural region, it is one of the major centers for the production of farm machinery and equipment. Also, it is the brewing center of the nation, reflecting its strong German heritage. To the south of Milwaukee is Kenosha, one of the leading automobile manufacturing centers outside the Southern Michigan Automotive District. In the same area is Racine, noted for its production of farm machinery, leather and leather products, and meat packing. Other cities of the Wisconsin part of the district produce electrical appliances, ships and boats, aluminum products, paper, and a wide variety of other manufactured items.

The Indiana-Ohio District. This district includes southwestern Ohio, southeastern Indiana, and adjacent parts of Kentucky. The greatest concentration of manufacturing in the district is in southwestern Ohio in the Miami Valley and on the Ohio River at Cincinnati. The Miami Valley produces a wide range of manufactured products, including iron and steel, with blast furnaces at Middletown and New Miami, machine tools, aircraft, computers and calculators, cash registers, and a variety of other products that require skilled labor. The major centers of the Miami Valley are Dayton, the largest; Hamilton, with paper and paper-making machinery a specialty; and Middletown, with its steel mill and diversified machinery production.

Cincinnati is the major city of the district and the largest manufacturing center on the Ohio River downstream from Pittsburgh. The early importance of Cincinnati as a pork-packing center has been mentioned, along with other early manufacturing that included cotton spinning, pottery, glass making, distilling, and steamboat building. In modern-day Cincinnati these old industries have been eclipsed by a highly diversified manufacturing complex that includes machine tools, auto parts, electrical equipment, and aircraft engines, to name a few examples. The Ohio River was the lifeline of the city in the early days. Although the river is no longer the dominating factor in the city's development, it still is important as an avenue of transport for Cincinnati's manufactured products.

No other area of the Indiana-Ohio District has a concentration of industry comparable to that of the Miami Valley. Rather, the industrial centers are isolated from one another by essentially agricultural lands. Chief among these outlying cities is Indianapolis, with its diversified manufacturing establishments producing fabricated metal products, food products, chemicals, and drugs. Other important Indiana cities in the Indiana-Ohio District are Fort Wayne, Muncie, and Anderson. To the east of the Miami Valley complex is Columbus, Ohio, a center of state government and education as well as diversified manufacturing. South of the Ohio River is Louisville, Kentucky, with its historic distilling industry, cigarette factories, and chemical plants. A recent addition to the Louisville manufacturing establishment is the world's largest household appliance plant, built and operated by the General Electric Company and employing some 10,000 workers. In addition to these larger centers, there are a number of smaller centers scattered throughout the district, such as Springfield, Fort Wayne, Lima, and Muncie.

MANUFACTURING CENTERS
NOT INCLUDED IN DISTRICTS

Outside the major manufacturing districts outlined on Figure 8 there are three major centers and a number of lesser centers of considerable importance to manufacturing in the North Central States. The major centers of manufacturing in this group are St. Louis, Kansas City, and Minneapolis-St. Paul. The lesser centers include several located in southwestern Michigan and northern Indiana, between the Southern Michigan Automotive District and the Chicago-Milwaukee District, and, in some respects, these functions as adjuncts to both districts. Among these cities are Grand Rapids, Kalamazoo, and South Bend. Another group of smaller manufacturing cities is found at the western margin of the North American Manufacturing Region in northern Illinois, southern Wisconsin, and eastern Iowa. These cities produce a variety of manufactured products with food products, farm machinery, and other light, diversified manufacturing.

Des Moines. Des Moines, Iowa, offers a good example of the types of manufacturing found in these cities. Not only is Des Moines a manufacturing center, but it is the state capital and the second most important center for the insurance industry after Hartford, Connecticut. A wide variety of manufacturing is found in the city including farm machinery, automobile tires, cement, meat packing, metal fabrication, and prefabricated building materials. It is also a major publishing and printing center. The Meredith Publishing Company, publishers of *Better Homes and Gardens* and *Successful Farming* magazines, is one of the largest combined publishing and printing establishments in the country. Des Moines recently was selected as the North American operations center for the Massey-Ferguson implement-manufacturing company, an operation formerly centered in Toronto. The company purchased an abandoned aircraft plant in the city and has converted it to the production of farm machinery.

St. Louis. The St. Louis metropolitan area, located in Missouri and Illinois, ranks ninth among manufacturing centers in the United States in terms of employees in manufacturing. St. Louis is a major transportation hub for traffic moving west and southwest and ranks second only to Chicago as a railroad center. Its manufacturing structure is more diversified than that of any other large American city except Philadelphia, with no single industry dominating the scene.[3] Transportation equipment is the largest single industry, but only by a slight margin.

On the Illinois side of the Mississippi River are the cities of East St. Louis, Granite City, Alton, and Belleville. Granite City is the center for primary iron and steel, and the area as a whole produces a variety of products, including electrical equipment, chemicals, drugs, petroleum products, etc. An important chemical center is located at Monsanto, Illinois, within the St. Louis metropolitan area. The Illinois side of the river accounts for about one-fourth of the manufacturing of the total metropolitan area of St. Louis.

Kansas City. Greater Kansas City includes Kansas City, Missouri, and Kansas City, Kansas, and is sometimes called the "Gateway to the Southwest." Because of its strategic location at the eastern margin of the Great Plains, it has developed as the major commercial and manufacturing center for the great agricultural area lying to the west of the Missouri River. It is the market center for the grains of the central and southern Great Plains and has developed as the continent's major flour-milling center. Its livestock market is one of the largest, and the meat-packing industry is of major importance. The city also produces farm machinery for the highly mechanized grain farms of the plains, and is the major center for the distribution of farm machinery of the United States. However, not all of the farm machinery marketed through Kansas

[3] Alexander, John W., *Economic Geography,* Prentice-Hall, Englewood Cliffs, 1963, p. 140.

City is manufactured there. Other industries include petroleum refining, chemicals, and a variety of food-processing and metal-working industries.

Minneapolis-St. Paul. The location of the Minneapolis-St. Paul metropolitan area in relation to the northern Great Plains is comparable to that of Kansas City to the central and southern Great Plains. Like Kansas City, it has developed as a supplier of agricultural machinery to the spring wheat region to the west, and as a processing center for the grain and other agricultural products from the region. Like Kansas City, it is one of the major flour-milling centers of the United States. Traditionally, the city of Minneapolis has been oriented to the commercial grain farming areas to the west, while St. Paul has looked northward to the forest industries of the upper Great Lakes and eastward to the dairy farming areas. Consequently, food processing leads the list of the diversified industries of Minneapolis, while St. Paul is an important center for paper products, abrasives, adhesives, and motor-vehicle assembly. The Minneapolis-St. Paul area is also one of the leading transportation centers of the nation, being served by a number of railroads and the Mississippi River barge traffic. Other industries produce, among other things, electrical equipment, linseed oil, heating equipment, and fertilizers.

Other Manufacturing Centers. In addition to the major manufacturing centers considered above, there are many smaller centers throughout the North Central States. Almost every city and town has some form of manufacturing, and it is the goal of all local governments and Chambers of Commerce to attract industry to the communities, regardless of size or location. Several areas should at least be mentioned. These include Wichita, a major center for aircraft manufacturing; Omaha, the major meat packer of the nation; and Denver and adjacent parts of the Colorado Piedmont, a center of light, diversified manufacturing that includes scientific instruments, mining equipment, and the primary iron and steel industry of Pueblo.

THE ROLE OF TRANSPORTATION

Transportation has been emphasized as a major adjunct to agriculture, mining, and manufacturing. Without dependable means of transporting the products of the land to the processing centers, and the finished products to the market, the economy of the North Central States could not function. Fortunately, the lack of major topographic barriers has made it relatively easy for an excellent land transportation network to develop. Railroads are the major carriers of bulk items and finished products, while a dense network of highways supplements the rail network. Water transportation serves much of the area through the Great Lakes Waterway and the St. Lawrence Seaway, and the Mississippi-Ohio-Missouri River system is gaining in importance. A dense network of pipelines spans the midcontinent carrying the products of the oil and gas fields from within the area and from surrounding areas to the refining centers. The opening of the St. Lawrence Seaway to ocean-going vessels in 1959 added a new dimension to the transportation and marketing situation of the Midwest, a role that should be considered in more detail.

The St. Lawrence Seaway. The Great Lakes Waterway has long figured importantly in the development of the North Central States. Stretching from the rich iron-ore deposits of the Lake Superior Uplands and the rich agricultural interior of the continent, to the industrial east with its dense population and vast resources of high-grade bituminous coal, the waterway has facilitated the rapid development of the region as a whole. Now the completion of the St. Lawrence Seaway makes it possible for ocean commerce to penetrate to the very heart of the North American continent.

With the completion of a 27-foot channel from Lake Ontario to Montreal, the Great Lakes were opened to world markets by direct ocean transportation on a large scale. Prior to the Seaway, only the smallest ocean-going vessels could reach the Great Lakes. However, in spite of the great enthusiasm which prevailed when the Seaway was opened, the tonnage of cargo carried during the first seven years of operation fell considerably short of expectations. However, the steady increase during each operational season, although not spectacular, gives reason for more optimistic expectations for the future, particularly as lake-port facilities are improved.

To date, the major part of the commodities shipped have been bulk items—mainly iron ore and grain. This is essentially the same type of cargo that characterized the Great Lakes Waterway before the Seaway was completed. Prior to the opening of the Seaway, these bulk commodities were destined for the internal markets of Canada and the United States, or for export via the eastern Atlantic ports. Today, the interior of the continent can ship its products directly to foreign markets for the first time. Grain and grain products have accounted for a major share of the tonnage for export, accounting for 70 percent of the total in 1961, and 81 percent in 1964. Animal products accounted for another 1.5 to 2.5 percent. Most of the remaining tonnage has been manufactured items and mine products, especially coal from the eastern end of the Great Lakes. The annual traffic for the six-year period 1959–1964 is summarized in Table 13.

The export picture on the St. Lawrence Seaway was summarized in the *Monthly Review* of the Federal Reserve Bank of Minneapolis for November, 1965, as follows:

> The kind of products shipped from Great Lakes ports indicates that the Seaway route was utilized principally to place midwest agriculture, in both the United States and Canada, in a better competitive position in world grain markets. The export breakdown indicates, however, that manufacturers in the Great Lakes region did not utilize the route as an aid in opening up new foreign markets for their products.[4]

[4] Federal Reserve Bank of Minneapolis, "The St. Lawrence Seaway—first 7 years," *Monthly Review*, November, 1965, pp. 3–4.

TABLE 13

Annual Traffic on the St. Lawrence Seaway by Principal Types of Commodities, 1959–1964
(thousands of cargo tons)

Years	Grains	Animal Products	Mine Products	Manufactures and Misc.	Forest Products	Package Freight	Total
1959	7,375.3	128.1	8,153.7	3,896.3	295.1	503.1	20,351.7
1960	8,220.5	224.8	6,476.5	4,549.4	284.4	554.9	20,310.3
1961	10,674.3	277.2	6,089.9	5,553.9	206.3	616.1	23,417.7
1962	11,333.8	307.4	8,190.0	4,887.9	252.4	622.2	25,593.6
1963	13,814.0	404.9	10,307.8	5,551.4	310.7	554.1	30,942.9
1964	16,940.6	540.0	14,172.7	6,694.3	336.5	625.0	39,309.0

Source: Federal Reserve Bank of Minneapolis, *Monthly Review*, November, 1965, p. 3.

Direct ocean transportation also opened the Great Lakes ports to foreign producers. A great increase of iron-ore shipments from Venezuela, Liberia, and Sweden did not materialize as had been expected. Imports into the lower Great Lakes ports of the North Central States consisted mainly of iron ore from eastern Canada. However, the shift to low-grade ores in the Lake Superior iron ranges has resulted in a lag in the imports of Canadian ores in recent years. Other commodities arriving at lake ports from abroad consisted principally of newsprint, pig iron, and fuel oil. In 1964, the total tonnage of iron ore amounted to 2,051,000 tons, while other imports totaled only 770,000 tons.

Railroads and Highways. The role of railroads in the growth of the North Central States already has been emphasized. The great rail network still functions to move raw materials to the processing centers and the finished goods to the consumers. But in recent decades the mileage of roalroads has actually decreased. Many small towns have lost their rail service, and abandoned stations and railroad rights-of-way are a common feature of the landscape. This reduction of rail service, particularly for short hauls, has been replaced by truck service, which is much more flexible for local deliveries. In fact, most of the major rail lines have subsidiary trucking lines to facilitate deliveries from rail centers to local areas, while retaining the more profitable long-haul traffic.

The rapid growth of the highway network has made trucking a major competitor of the railroads, as well as a supplement to rail service. Highway transport is no longer reserved for the short haul, but commodities may move great distances by truck. In addition, the popularity of the private automobile has caused a major reduction in the use of railroads by passengers. Most lines are cutting back on passenger service and would like to eliminate it altogether. The traveler not wishing to drive his automobile often is left with a choice of traveling by bus or by air.

The automobile also has brought about a deterioration of public transportation in the metropolitan areas. In the North Central States, where the automobile gained early acceptance, the decline of public transportation has been more rapid than in the more crowded eastern cities. Even the small towns have their parking problems, and moderate-sized cities are finding it increasingly difficult to supply public conveyance for the dwindling clientele of the urban bus lines.

8 *The Heartland and the American Scene*

IT is appropriate to end this study of the heartland of the North American continent where we began, by emphasizing the vital contributions of this area to the total economic strength of the United States. No other area of comparable size has contributed so handsomely to the well-being of a nation in such a variety of ways, from the products of its rich agricultural land and its mines and forests, to its great industrial complex. The varied resources of the North Central States have formed the basis for the development of a viable regional economy, with attendant high living standards for a majority of the people of the area, and have contributed as well to the strong economic position of the nation as a whole.

However, in considering the significance of the region in the national scene, we cannot forget its problems. Prosperity and poverty form rather definite geographic patterns in the North Central States, but statistics for the region as a whole tend to mask the areas of economic stress as well as those of economic well-being. Metropolitan areas appear as concentrations of high productivity, high income, and material wealth, while they hide slums with degrading poverty. The patterns of prosperity and of poverty are a significant part of the geography of the North Central States.

We would also be amiss in our treatment of the area if we forgot that the politics of a region of this size and population have a profound effect on the political life of the nation. Sectionalism in American politics has become less a factor than it was in the past,

139

but vestiges of the old regional patterns of politics emerge upon a closer study of the voting patterns of the region. Recent trends in the historic political competition between urban and rural forces, brought about by major shifts in population, are major factors in shaping the political geography of the region.

REGIONAL CONTRIBUTIONS TO THE NATIONAL ECONOMY

Without the North Central States the United States would be a quite different country in terms of its resource base. A comparative study of the United States and the Soviet Union indicates that the lack of an extensive area comparable to the American Corn Belt, especially in terms of climate, has contributed to the problems of Soviet agriculture. The intense interest of Soviet agricultural experts in the feed-grain and livestock economy of the Corn Belt, as evidenced by numerous visits of these experts to Iowa, points up the weakness of Soviet agriculture in terms of feed grains for meat production. Also, the failure of the Soviet corn-growing program and a reemphasis on wheat production under the new regime underlines that country's lack of extensive corn-growing areas comparable to the Feed Grain and Livestock region of the United States. Unlike many industrial countries with a more limited resource base, the United States is able to produce substantially all of its basic food needs, importing chiefly luxury foods such as tropical fruits, coffee, and sugar.

Although the degree of self-sufficiency that is found in agriculture is lacking, mineral resources are large, and the North Central States contribute an important share of the country's total. Of particular strategic importance is the iron ore of the Lake Superior region. For purposes of economy, we have turned more and more to foreign sources of iron ore as the rich, easily mined ores of the iron ranges have been exhausted. Now, with the rapid development of enrichment techniques for the vast reserves of low-grade taconite ores of the Lake Superior area, this trend seems to have been slowed and conceivably could be reversed if world political conditions made it necessary.

The area's contribution in terms of mineral fuels has been equally significant. The North Central States still have vast reserves of bituminous coal and almost untapped reserves of subbituminous coal and lignite. With new sources of energy from atomic power on the horizon, it seems unlikely that these lower grades of fuels ever will be widely utilized. Although the area's contribution to the supply of petroleum and natural gas has been less spectacular, it has been significant.

The list of other minerals contributed to the regional and national economy is a long one. It includes the production of the world's leading lead-mining district of Missouri and the zinc of the Driftless Area and the Tri-State Area. Again, if conditions, either political or economic, warranted, the zinc output could be vastly increased by tapping low-grade reserves. The area has the nation's leading gold mine at Lead, South Dakota, the operation of which may cease unless the price of gold rises or ways to make mining more economical are found.

Forest resources are modest in the North Central States, although at one time the Lake States portion of the region was the nation's major lumber supplier. This is, in part, due to the fact that the suitability of large areas for cultivation has resulted in the wholesale removal of forests. The gradual increase in forest planting and improvement in forest management in areas less suited to modern commercial farming may result in an increase in the region's contribution of forest products.

We have emphasized that the North Central States contain a major share of the territory occupied by the American Manufacturing Region. The primary iron and steel and metals industries of the Pittsburgh-Cleveland District and the Gary area furnish materials for a host of other manufacturers in the area, chief among them the automobile manufacturers. The agricultural heartland supplies raw materials in the form of grain, dairy products, meat, and other commodities to the food-processing industries. The highly mechanized agriculture, in turn, furnishes a booming market for the products of the farm-machinery makers and for a growing list of agricultural chemicals and fertilizers. Finally, a prosperous population furnishes a market for the ultimate products of manufacturing, the consumer goods and services.

PROBLEMS OF AGRICULTURE

In spite of the overall prosperity of the North Central States, major problems do exist. Agriculture is in a period of transition in which the less-successful farmers are being forced off the land through economic pressures, and are moving to more profitable employment in the urban centers. Sometimes this transition from rural to urban life creates problems for the displaced persons as well as for the cities. Often, the less-successful of the farming population are less well-equipped to take full advantage of the opportunities offered by urban living—witness the plight of many immigrants into the northern cities from the rural South.

The farmer who stays on the land is faced with a price-cost squeeze between the price he receives for his products and the cost of the machinery, seed, chemicals, and fertilizers he must use to be successful as a modern farmer. The survival of the family-operated farm as the backbone of American agriculture is now in question. Can the small, independent operator survive the cost-price squeeze and the increasing demands for capital, or is the large, corporation-owned, factory-type farm destined to replace him? Some agricultural economists believe that the family farm will survive, but that the average size will increase to perhaps two to three times its present size. In Iowa, this would mean an average farm size of from 400 to 600 acres, the size of some family farms today. These same agricultural economists believe that larger operating units are feasible, but will not be more efficient in terms of price per unit produced. If this be the case, the family farm will probably survive, but in a larger and more efficient form.

Agricultural surpluses seemed less a problem in 1966 than they did in the past decade. Reserves of corn and wheat were at a low level, and no surplus existed in soybeans. Increasing exports were part of the reason for the diminished farm surpluses. While acreage reduction was the rule in previous farm programs, these programs were replaced by an emphasis on increased production. In the fall of 1966, the Department of Agriculture announced plans to call for an increase in the acreage of corn, and there was real concern about a potential shortage of soybeans and the low level of wheat reserves. By the end of 1967, surpluses were again a problem.

THE PATTERN OF PROSPERITY

A map of the counties of the United States in economic distress is largely blank in the core areas of the North Central States. Only a few counties in the Midland Feed Region (Corn Belt) and the Great Plains fall into the category of "poverty pockets." Only the fringing areas to the north and south have continuous blocks of economically distressed counties. Iowa, in the heart of the Corn Belt, has only two counties so designated.

That the North Central States is a prosperous area is borne out by statistics on personal income by states for 1965. All but two states lying wholly within the region ranked in the upper half of the 50 states in per capita personal income (the exceptions: North Dakota ranked 36 and South Dakota ranked 42). Illinois was first in the region and fifth nationally with a per capita income of $3,245, compared with a national figure of $2,742. All North Central States east of the Mississippi River except Wisconsin ranked above the national average, a reflection of the greater industrialization and higher wages associated with the large metropolitan areas.

Agriculture is prosperous throughout a large part of the North Central States in spite of those problems that have been described. However, these are, for the most part, problems of successful farm operators. An indication of the general high level of farming can be seen in the distribution of "first-class" farms as defined by the

Bureau of the Census. A first-class farm is one from which gross sales of $40,000 or more are made annually. According to the 1959 Census of Agriculture the North Central States had about one-third of the nation's total of these first-class farms, with Iowa and Illinois accounting for almost one-half of the regional total. As would be expected, a major share of these super farms were in the Central Prairie Subregion of the Midland Feed Region (Figure 5).

The area also had less than its share of the lowest economic category of farms—those with gross sales of less than $2,500—with only about 5 percent of the farms falling into this category, against almost 10 percent nationally. In contrast, the East South Central Census Region (Kentucky, Tennessee, Alabama, and Mississippi) had over 20 percent of its farms in the lowest category in 1959.

THE PATTERN OF POVERTY

Economically distressed counties of the North Central States fall into three major geographic areas: (1) the Southern Transition including the Ozarks, Interior Low Plateaus, the Appalachians of southeastern Ohio and fringing areas of the Central Lowlands; (2) the Cutover Area of northern Minnesota, Wisconsin, and Michigan; and (3) counties of the northern Great Plains containing major Indian reservations, particularly in the Dakotas and Montana. Poverty is in part related to the poor resource base of the areas and the attendant lack of education, as well as to other socio-economic factors.

In the Southern Transition the topography and poor soils limit agricultural productivity and farm income. In some areas of the southern border, coal mining has been important; the decline in employment in the mines and the reluctance of the ex-miners to move to areas of greater economic opportunity have left a residue of poverty-stricken peoples. This area is essentially a northern extension of the pattern of rural poverty that has been characteristic of the South.

The Cutover Area of the northern Great Lakes also has limited potential for agriculture. Good soils are scarce and interspersed with poor soils so that an individual farm generally has only a small portion of land that is productive. Lumbering and mining brought most of the settlers into the region and destructive logging practices exhausted the forest resource and left the immigrant workers to fend for themselves in a land of limited opportunity. Population densities are low in this region and the total number of people in the poverty category is probably considerably less than in the southern border areas where population densities are greater.

The Indian reservations of the northern Great Plains are a special case in the pattern of poverty in the North Central States. Not only were the lands set aside as reservations generally of low quality, but the Indian peoples have not fully recovered from the destruction of their tribal societies. Economic opportunities on the reservations are extremely limited, and lack of education and skills makes it difficult for the Indian to move. Solution of the Indian problem is a difficult one because it is obscured by the isolation of most Indian lands from the mainstream of American life. The plight of the Indian is seldom obvious to most Americans, in contrast to the plight of the Negro and the slum dweller, whose problems are constantly brought to public attention.

The distribution of economically distressed counties masks much of the poverty which is obscured by averages and median incomes. All metropolitan areas have their slums and economically depressed neighborhoods. The influx of migrants from the areas of declining rural population, particularly the Negro from the South, has intensified the problem of urban poverty. Also, isolated areas of rural poverty and individual poverty-stricken farms can be found even in the best agricultural areas.

THE PATTERN OF POLITICS

There was a time when sectionalism was the decisive factor in American politics. Each party was able to count on certain "safe" areas to deliver the vote. In this pattern of sectionalism most of the states in the North Central States were Republican. Certain counties, however, were traditionally Democratic, particularly where immigrants from the South and their descendants formed "Little Dixies" or where recent immigrants from eastern and southern Europe gave their loyalty to the Democratic Party. The old sectionalism is breaking down, as evidenced by recent elections, although much of the rural Midwest is almost as Republican as the Solid South is Democratic.

In the North Central States, as in the remainder of the country outside the South, the shift in the balance of population from country to city has given an advantage to the Democrats, particularly in presidential elections where total votes in a state are the deciding factor. However, if counties are considered, the normal Republicanism of a large part of the region becomes apparent (Table 14). Except in disaster years for the Republican Party, such as 1932 and 1936 and the Goldwater debacle of 1964, Republican counties have been in the majority. The fact that the Republicans can win a majority of counties and a minority of states—for example, in 1948—indicates the concentration of Democratic strength in the large urban counties. This also explains why most Republican politicians favor preservation of area representation over the "one man, one vote" philosophy of the Supreme Court. It also explains why many states have legislatures that are Republican-dominated although they may give majorities to Democratic presidential candidates and governors.

If voting patterns of counties are considered for individual elections, certain patterns emerge. In all recent presidential elections the counties corresponding to the Cutover Area of northern Minnesota, Michigan, and Wisconsin have been almost solidly Democratic, even in Democratic disaster years such as 1952 and 1956. This pattern of Democratic loyalty also can be seen in east-central Missouri, the eastern Ozarks, and the Missouri Bootheel. However, it is interesting to note that the eastern Ozark area of Missouri gave a majority to Nixon over Kennedy in 1960, perhaps due to the religious issue, which was intense in the fundamentalist Protestant sectors of the

TABLE 14

Counties and States [1] of the North Central States Carried by Major Political Parties, 1932–1964 *

Presidential Election	Republican Counties	Democratic Counties	Republican States	Democratic States	Victorious Party for President
1932	121	934	0	12	Democrats
1936	318	920	0	12	Democrats
1940	793	293	7	5	Democrats
1944	818	238	8	4	Democrats
1948	661	395	6	6	Democrats
1952	998	67	12	0	Republicans
1956	964	92	11	1	Republicans
1960	916	137	8	4	Democrats
1964	173	883	0	12	Democrats

[1] Does not include Colorado, Montana, and Wyoming, which lie partially outside the North Central States.

* *Source:* Based on compilations by Dr. Paul Willis, Political Science Department, Drake University.

Southern Transition. In 1964, Goldwater lost all states in the North Central States, but on a county basis he showed his greatest strength in the sparsely populated Great Plains, where he had considerable appeal to the ranchers. Goldwater carried most of the counties of western Nebraska, although he lost the more populous counties in the southeast. He also had a higher percentage of the popular vote in Nebraska (47.4 percent) than in any other state of the North Central States.

The pattern of voting by states is more in line with the national pattern (Table 15). In seven of the ten presidential elections from 1928 to 1964, a majority of the North Central States went to the winning candidate. Two states, Illinois and Minnesota, agreed with the national outcome in every one of the ten elections. Two other states, Missouri and Montana, differed only once; and Michigan, Ohio, Wisconsin, and Wyoming differed from the national results only twice in the ten elections. All fifteen states of the area voted for the victorious candidate in five of the ten elections.

Traditionally, the continental interior has been a stronghold of isolationism. Prior to World War I and in the decades preceding World War II, isolationism reached its peak. As Samuel Lubell has pointed out in his in-depth studies of American politics, much of the isolationist sentiment had an ethnic base.[1] This tendency to isolationism was exploited by the Republican Party, especially the conservative wing represented by the editorial policies of the *Chicago Tribune*. In World War I, many German-Americans and Scandinavian-Americans were pro-German and anti-British, as were many Irish-Americans. This led to hysterical moves on the part of many other Americans to eradicate everything German from the American scene and led to persecution of many German-Americans. At least a part of the isolationism of the 1920's and 1930's was a reaction of the German-Americans against this persecution, which they long remembered. Much of the support in Wisconsin for La Follette and for the isolationist Non-Partisan League came from the

[1] Lubell, Samuel, *The Future of American Politics,* Harper, New York, 1951, 1952, pp. 129–157.

Table 15

Majority Vote for President by States of the North Central States, 1928 to 1964

	1928	1932	1936	1940	1944	1948	1952	1956	1960	1964	Years not Following National Trend
United States	R	D	D	D	D	D	R	R	D	D	
Colorado (6)	R	D	D	R*	D	D	R	R	R*	D	3
Illinois (26)	R	D	D	D	D	D	R	R	D	D	0
Indiana (13)	R	D	D	R*	R*	R*	R	R	R*	D	4
Iowa (9)	R	D	D	R*	R*	D	R	R	R*	D	3
Kansas (7)	R	D	D	R*	R*	R*	R	R	R*	D	4
Michigan (21)	R	D	D	R*	D	R*	R	R	D	D	2
Minnesota (10)	R	D	D	D	D	D	R	R	D	D	0
Missouri (12)	R	D	D	D	D	D	R	D*	D	D	1
Montana (4)	R	D	D	D	R*	D	R	R	R*	D	1
Nebraska (5)	R	D	D	R*	R*	R*	R	R	R*	D	4
N. Dakota (4)	R	D	D	R*	R*	R*	R	R	R*	D	4
Ohio (26)	R	D	D	D	R*	D	R	R	R*	D	2
S. Dakota (4)	R	D	D	R*	R*	R*	R	R	R*	D	4
Wisconsin (12)	R	D	D	D	R*	D	R	R	R*	D	2
Wyoming (3)	R	D	D	D	R*	D	R	R	R*	D	2
Number of States for Winning Cand.	15	15	15	7	4	9	15	14	4	15	

Number in parentheses after state indicates electoral votes, 1964.
* Election in which state did not follow the national trend.

basically conservative Germans, Scandinavians, and Russian-Germans, as well as from the economic liberals who distrusted the big money interests of the East.

The fact that isolationism is probably misnamed is indicated by the fact that many of the same areas that were isolationist where Germany and Great Britain were concerned, are now "hawks" in relationships with the U.S.S.R. and China, and in Vietnam. In other words, isolationism in the Midwest has tended to be selective.

Contrary to the belief of many in the East, and in the cities of the Midwest, the writer has found that many farmers have a world point of view which equals or exceeds that of the average urban dweller. This world awareness was illustrated by the friendly reception accorded the Soviet farm delegation and Nikita Khrushchev in Iowa. This world awareness should increase as American agricultural products move in increasing quantities into the world markets.

The decline of the historic power of the rural minority in American politics already has been alluded to. Most of the states of the so-called farm bloc are actually more urban than rural, and the reapportionment of state legislatures and the national House of Representatives will shift the political power to the cities. The favorable political climate for agriculture that has been traditional in American government is being replaced by a greater concern in Washington for the neglected urban problems of our major cities. What effect these changes will have on farm legislation pertaining to rural problems, and on legislation relating to urban problems, remains to be seen. Whatever the outcome of this shift in political power, it will have wide-ranging effects on both the rural and the urban peoples of the North Central States.

The future role of the Democratic and Republican parties in the North Central States seems somewhat unclear. Changes in the geographic distribution of people undoubtedly will have far-reaching effects on voting patterns within the area. The rural Midwest, including the small towns, has been traditionally a stronghold of Republicanism. On the other hand, the large metropolitan areas have followed the pattern of cities in other parts of the country and have tended to vote Democratic. The decline in rural population would seem to favor the Democrats, as would the influx of southern Negroes into the large northern cities. Also, the farmer no longer can be counted on to vote the straight Republicanism of his fore-fathers. No group, with the possible exception of the Negroes, is so conscious of the role of government in its welfare, and so ready to change party allegiance for self-interest. However, the rapid growth of the suburbs, reflecting the improved economic status of the urban population, would seem to favor the Republicans.

The last two national elections further confused the issue of regional party allegiance. In the presidential election of 1964, all of the North Central States gave President Johnson and the Democrats large majorities. In Iowa the Democratic ticket had its greatest victory in recent times, capturing the governorship and most elec-tive state offices, and gaining a majority in the State Legislature and the national Congress. In 1966, the tide was reversed and the Re-publicans again gained control of the State Legislature and replaced the Democratic majority in Congress. However, Democrats were elected as Governor and Lieutenant Governor. The same general pattern of Democratic victory in 1964 and Republican resurgence in 1966 was characteristic of most of the other states of the area. One thing seems certain: neither of the major parties can count with certainty on the votes of the diverse population groups of the North Central States.

THE FUTURE

The North Central States will continue to play a vital role in all phases of American life. The rate of growth of the area, especially of the less industrialized states, will probably be slower than for the periphery of the continent, particularly the West Coast. In spite of this, the well-established agricultural and industrial base will make this lesser rate of growth very significant in terms of absolute in-creases. The North Central States are destined to remain function-ally, as well as geographically, the heartland of the continent.

Selected Bibliography

Akin, Wallace E., "Can the Russians Develop a Corn Belt?", *Successful Farming,* September, 1956.

Alexander, John W., *Economic Geography,* Prentice-Hall, Englewood Cliffs, 1963.

Auer, L. E., Heady, E. O., and Conklin, F., "Influence of 'Crop Technology' on Yields," *Iowa Farm Science,* March, 1966, Vol. 20, No. 9, Iowa State Univ., Ames, pp. 13–16.

Barrows, Harlan H. (Edited by Koelsch, W. H.), *Lectures on the Historical Geography of the United States as Given in 1933,* Department of Geography Research Paper No. 77, University of Chicago, 1962.

Billington, Ray Allen, *Westward Expansion,* Macmillan, New York, 1960.

Brown, Ralph H., *Historical Geography of the United States,* Harcourt Brace, New York, 1958.

Center for Agricultural and Economic Development, *Weather and Our Food Supply,* CAED Report 20, Iowa State Univ., Ames, 1964.

Federal Reserve Bank of Kansas City, "Grazing in the Bluestem Belt," *Monthly Review,* July–August, 1965, Kansas City, Missouri.

Federal Reserve Bank of Minneapolis, "The St. Lawrence Seaway—first 7 years," *Monthly Review,* November, 1965, pp. 3–4.

Fenneman, Nevin M., *Physiography of the Western United States,* McGraw-Hill, New York, 1931.

———, *Physiography of the Eastern United States,* McGraw-Hill, New York, 1938.

Goodrich, Carter (Ed.), *Canals in American Economic Development,* Columbia Univ. Press, New York, 1961.

Hair, Dwight, *The Economic Importance of Timber in the United States,* U.S. Department of Agriculture, Forest Service, Misc. Pub. 941, Superintendent of Documents, Government Printing Office, Washington, D.C., 1963.

Hart, John Fraser, "The Changing Distribution of the American Negro," *Annals of the Association of American Geographers,* Vol. 50, No. 3, Sept., 1960, pp. 242–266.

Higbee, Edward, *American Agriculture: Geography, Resources, Conservation,* Wiley, New York, 1958.

———, *Farms and Farmers in an Urban Age,* Twentieth Century Fund, New York, 1963.

Iowa State College, Agricultural Extension Service, *Sawmills in Iowa,* Ames, 1953.

Iowa State University Center for Agricultural and Economic Adjustment, *Dynamics of Land Use—Needed Adjustment,* Iowa State Univ. Press, Ames, 1961.

Iowa State University Center for Agricultural and Economic Adjustment, *Problems and Policies of American Agriculture,* Iowa State Univ. Press, Ames, 1959.

Kerr, Donald, "The St. Lawrence Seaway and Trade on the Great Lakes, 1958–1963," *The Canadian Geographer,* VII, 4, 1964, pp. 188–196.

Kollmorgen, W. M., and Simonette, D. S., "Grazing Operations in the Flint Hills-Bluestem Pastures of Chase County, Kansas," *Annals of the Association of American Geographers,* Vol. 55, No. 2, June, 1966, pp. 260–290.

Lounsbury, John F., "Industrial Development in the Ohio Valley," *The Journal of Geography,* Vol. LX, No. 6, Sept., 1961, pp. 253–262.

Lubell, Samuel, *The Future of American Politics,* Harper, New York, 1951, 1952.

McCarty, H. H., *The Geographic Basis of American Economic Life,* Harper, New York, 1940.

———, "Iowa and the American Manufacturing Belt," *Iowa Business Digest,* Winter, 1960, Bureau of Business and Economic Research, Univ. of Iowa, Iowa City.

Mendel, Joseph J., *Trends in Pulpwood Production in the United States,* Technical Paper 188, U.S. Department of Agriculture, Forest Service, Central States Experiment Station, Columbus, Ohio, April, 1962.

The National Farm Institute, *What's Ahead for the Family Farm?*, Iowa State University Press, Ames, 1966.

Riley, Charles M., *Our Mineral Resources,* Wiley, New York, 1959.

Soth, Lauren, *An Embarrassment of Plenty: Agriculture in Affluent America,* Crowell, New York, 1965.

Technical Committee on Soil Survey, *Soils of the North Central Region of the United States,* North Central Region Pub. No. 76, Agricultural Experiment Station, Univ. of Wisconsin, Madison, 1960.

Thornbury, William H., *Regional Geomorphology of the United States,* Wiley, New York, 1965.

U.S. Department of the Interior, *Mineral Facts and Problems,* Bull. 630, Bureau of Mines, 1965 Edition, Superintendent of Documents, Government Printing Office, Washington, D.C., 1965.

U.S. Department of Agriculture, *Climate and Man,* 1941 Yearbook of Agriculture, Superintendent of Documents, Government Printing Office, Washington, D.C., 1941.

————, *The Balance Sheet for Agriculture,* Agricultural Information Bull. No. 290, Sept., 1965, Superintendent of Documents, Government Printing Office, Washington, D.C., 1965.

————, *Changes in Farm Production Efficiency, A Summary Report, 1962,* Statistical Bull. No. 233, Sept., 1962, Superintendent of Documents, Government Printing Office, Washington, D.C., 1962.

————, *Characteristics of the U.S. Population by Farm and Nonfarm Origin,* Economic and Statistical Analysis Division, Agricultural Economic Report No. 66, Superintendent of Documents, Government Printing Office, Washington, D.C., 1964.

————, Forest Service, *Forest Planting Practices in the Central United States,* Agricultural Handbook No. 247, Superintendent of Documents, Government Printing Office, Washington, D.C., December, 1963.

————, *Land,* 1958 Yearbook of Agriculture, Superintendent of Documents, Government Printing Office, Washington, D.C., 1958.

————, *Land Use and its Patterns in the United States,* Agricultural Handbook No. 153, Superintendent of Documents, Government Printing Office, Washington, D.C., 1959.

————, *Soil,* 1957 Yearbook of Agriculture, Superintendent of Documents, Government Printing Office, Washington, D.C., 1957.

Visher, Stephen S., *Climatic Atlas of the United States,* Harvard Univ. Press, Cambridge, Mass., 1954.

White, C. L., Foscue, E. J., and McKnight, T. L., *Regional Geography of Anglo-America,* 3rd ed., Prentice-Hall, Englewood Cliffs, 1964.

Index